Simply More Words from the Saddle

Scot Whitlock is a writer, author and editor of *CADENCE* cycling magazine, he writes predominately about cycling and its endless joys. This is his second book and follows on from the success of his first foray into literature with *Simple Words from the Saddle*.

Praise For

Simple Words from the Saddle

'Really enjoyed it, loved your style and some of the comments about things of interest' **Pauline Pittam**

'It's fab, definitely inspired to get my road bike built so I can have a few adventures' **Sophie Heaviside, Leamington Observer**

'Just started reading the book. Really enjoying the detail of each ride, can sort of picture in my head where you are' **Michael Lyons, Keen Cyclist**

Also by the author

Simple Words from the Saddle

Scot Whitlock

Simply More Words from the Saddle

Olympia Publishers
London

www.olympiapublishers.com
OLYMPIA PAPERBACK EDITION

A CIP catalogue record for this title is available from the British Library.

ISBN: 978-1-84897-722-8

(Olympia Publishers is part of Ashwell Publishing Ltd)

Published in 2016

Olympia Publishers
60 Cannon Street
London
EC4N 6NP

Printed in Great Britain

To my children, Noah, Eli, Rosie, Lauren and Evie,
follow your dreams.

Thanks to David Millar, Jess Varnish, Michelle Paget, Peter Wakefield, Olympia Publishers, Jenny Treadwell and my wife Sarah.

Contents

Preface

I have been amazed by the success of my first book, 'Simple Words from the Saddle'. It was always just a simple way of me remembering what I have done and where I had ventured. The older I get, the more I have had to accept that certain aspects of my life have changed significantly, grey hair has become increasingly prevalent, I somehow daily forget the location of my car or house keys, sometimes both. My children are growing at a rapid rate and I have recognised my body shape is slowly emerging into middle age.

Nevertheless, my passion for cycling has increased (if that is remotely possible) and has allowed me to move forward from the issues that modern daily life throws at us.

Since writing 'Simple Words from the Saddle', I am increasingly seeing cyclists wearing masks on the UK streets, and this isn't just on the usual urban streets but also in rural less populated areas. Is this a genuine concern? Is pollution at the level where it is logical to don masks to reduce the impact on health? Or are we being overcautious, especially in the suburbs and shires?

Research dictates that the levels of pollution created by vehicles in the UK is a concern, but not significant enough to implement measures like we see in certain parts of the world. Congestion and pollution sit together in this debate and with China and other eastern countries topping the list of the world's most congested and polluted cities, it's right for them to acknowledge the impact on health and take steps to reach a satisfactory resolution.

The UK's major cities are aware of the impact from congestion and are continually working with transport providers to promote the benefits of using public transport, or, with health providers, to highlight the positives of regular exercise and choosing walking or cycling as a great alternative to the car.

Locally and nationally through several initiatives and organisations (Sustrans, for example), the UK is vigorously pushing cycling and its benefits, both for the individual and the environment. In the long run, pollution is about education, time and mostly money. We all need to accept pollution abatement as an important factor in our lives and individually take steps to address ours and societies shortcomings. The first positive step is leave the car at home and jump on a bike, simple and effective.

My hope is eventually every UK household will have access to a bike with the prospect of our roads being over-run by two wheeled transportation. The car will become a mere memory of a bygone era. Anyhow, I accept this cycling nirvana is a long way off and can only be achieved with a coming together of all areas of society, road users or not!

On a plus I have to admit the public image of cycling has improved markedly over the past three years. The pastime was once marginal and somewhat poncy but since the legacy of the London Olympics and people's desire for a more healthy lifestyle, cycling has now become cool, chic and a good alternative to the gym. With the sport indeed on the up, why is it that cyclists are still vilified by everyone else for being dangerous, impatient, and occasionally down right obnoxious? Probably because a few of us are. I am not here to defend or praise good and bad examples of behaviour, but I recognise that in a large society you will get a mixture of both, and cycling is no different. I believe because cycling has made a seismic shift from the margins to the mainstream at a rapid speed, this has raised awareness of the effects of congestion and the need for sustainable transport with a more determined focus on the greener agenda. The cycling infrastructure is gradually invading all built up areas and will continue to provide a realistic resolution for town planners but it takes money, and lots of it, which is why I feel other road users dislike the increasing Lycra clad amongst us.

Unfortunately we are still a minority but we have accepted that the absolute right thing to do, is ride a bike, be it for fitness, commuting or just simple fun. We don't care if we are increasingly vulnerable as we pedal because riding is part of our lives, it's in our blood and hey, it's convenient, healthy, quick, relatively cheap and great fun. The unusual weird members of society are those that choose not to pedal, as they endlessly wait in traffic and unapologetically pollute the atmosphere with fuel guzzling SUV's.

I hope you enjoy the book

Happy Pedalling

The ultimate bike city bursting with a vibrant pragmatic approach to life and pedalling. (September 2014)

I knew the time would come when I would eventually travel to Amsterdam and jump on a bicycle, the city is synonymous with the bike, around every corner and in every crevice it breathes bikes. It's a cyclist's spiritual home, a temple to all things two wheeled.

My hope was to experience a bike utopia but my apprehension was evident as we boarded the Stena Line service from Harwich to the Hook of Holland. My concern was that my impression of the city as a laid-back, welcoming and tolerant place might just be a figment of my always positive imagination. I have always loved the idea of Amsterdam; its pragmatism is by far its greatest attraction. The Dutch had the first homosexual marriage, the red light district is regularly visited by families and it's synonymous with its relaxed approach to drugs, which infuriates most because in reality the liberal drugs policy hasn't curiously seen an increase in drug use. The plan was simple, immerse in all that Amsterdam had to offer, remarkable museums, contemporary galleries, an intricate network of canals and pulsating nightlife. I couldn't wait!

The ferry was to be our romantic base for the night, not me and my bike but me and my wife (who was my official photographer for the duration).

The cabin was bigger than I was expecting and we slept relatively well considering we were at sea. Over a delicious dinner the previous night, I interestingly read that, to behave like the native Amsterdammers, I should be on the constant look out for Gezellig which is fundamentally about creating an environment that allows good times to happen.

On the agenda would have to be an obligatory visit to one of the many independent cafés. There are an abundance of these infamous establishments dotted throughout the city, café-clubs, café-pubs and café-bars. Our base was on the Spuistraat with alluring views of the Singel Canal. On the cusp of the Jordaan area, it is a mass of grandiose canal houses decorated with resounding summer blooms. It was originally a working class area, home to the stone masons and construction workers, laidback and welcoming. Around every corner is concealed greenery, a secret verdant hideaway discreetly enjoying the rays of the sun. A flourishing art scene, artisan shops, modern boutique hotels and a plethora of enticing cafés and restaurants have transformed the Jordaan into a dynamic and affluent neighbourhood. The city canals celebrated 400 years last year and the old canal system forms an intricate semi-circle around the medieval part of the city, creating a harmonious blend of cutting edge design and simple naive beauty.

The city's architecture is influenced by gables, in spout, step, neck and bell styles. The opulent houses, which enjoy memorable vistas of the canals, impress not so much with their size but with their overall distinguishing features and character. The enthusiastic colours and warming façades of these predominately private dwellings gives Amsterdam a wealth of architectural marvels unsurpassable by no other city in Europe. I love taking photographs; they provide a unique portal to understand a place. What we often don't see initially becomes clear when you take the time to look and linger. The vivid colours of a building, the mundane enhanced by a simple action, the understated beauty of a fleeting moment of reality. Amsterdam's cityscape is the ideal canvas, full of visual clichés; it provides a contemporary mixture of chaotic movement and relaxing stillness that is created by the bike, the water and the sun-shaded back streets.

My first venture out on the bike took me to the southern part of the city. The bike is undeniably the best option to explore, especially the canal belt. Anyhow, a word of caution, there is a recognised problem with bike theft. There are plenty of bicycle rental outlets dotted throughout, which are happy to organise tours and assist with cycle maps, as well as the unmistakable bike hire. Crazy cycling is accepted, strangely it appears it is encouraged. Bikes zipping along tram lanes, cycle paths, pavements, the constant din of the overused bell foreboding danger. They have been described as the 'Silent Killers' and at times I nearly succumbed in a blur of pedal power. It's not about speed, it's about the history and affiliation the city has with the bike and its legacy. The bike is most indubitably King, long live the King!

After negotiating the trams and constant stream of cyclists, I arrived in front of the ornate gates of the Vondelpark, which is the most famous of the City's parks. It offers an abundance of ponds, gardens and resplendent tracks and footpaths. I halted by the memorial, the sun was strong and shade was at a premium. The facts and numbers on cycling in the city are astonishing and unquestionably something the UK should aspire to. There are an estimated 881,000 bikes and 58% of Amsterdammers use their bikes daily. In comparison there are only 263,000 cars with 37% movement of traffic being by car and 38% by bicycle. The maze of cycle paths total 400km, it's undeniably a city that's completely eclipsed by all things two wheeled. Cycling was accepted as the main method of navigating the city in the country's pre-World War II days and even played a role during the Nazi occupation of the city in the 1940s. It's believed the Germans hated Amsterdam cyclists with their blasé attitude full of bravado and anarchy. The locals purposely slowed up convoys and refused to give way to German vehicles. It gave the locals the opportunity to display their dissatisfaction towards the invaders and hinder their cause.

From the greenery I pedalled on towards the city's cultural heart. Once home to a stinky wax candle factory and marshy meadows, the Museum Quarter has been transformed into the City's most affluent area. Home to the Riksmuseum, Stedelijk Museum, Van Gogh Museum and a diverse array of boutique outlets and specialist artisan shops, which would adequately fuel any shopping spree.

The Rijksmusuem is massive and is believed to house over one million objects. Its dazzling ornate façade is best enjoyed from the peaceful serenity of the fastidiously manicured gardens opposite, the only sound was the sporadic rush of water from the contemporary water feature set in the heart of the greenery. As we approached the entrance I noticed several cyclists emerge from the interior. Amazingly a bicycle path has allowed pedestrians and cyclists a shortcut across the city ever since the museum was built. The path is in a tunnel, separating galleries and proving a nuisance to curators, but offering a unique opportunity for Amsterdam's cycle-loving citizens. Nevertheless, whilst the museum was closed for renovation there were calls for its permanent closure, the Rijksmuseum arguing it was a hazard to its visitors. At one point, there was a chance the city might have to hold a referendum before the City Council jumped in and decided that it would stay. Vigilance and compromise is key.

Inside the highlight and main attraction is the Rembrandt floor especially the world famous 'Night Watch' depicting the jovial bunch of civic guards, it was great to be able to sit looking at this masterpiece with the minimal distraction, apart from the occasional interloper (usually American) but my personal favourite is the 'Militia Company of District VIII under the command of Captain Roelof Bicker' by Bartholomeus van der Helst. The images so lifelike, the painter capturing every emotion and expression.

You can wander aimlessly in this rabbit warren of art. We stumbled on another high point, 'The library' which resembled a Harry Potter set, the only modern intrusion was the necessity for connectivity with several of a fruity brand of devices juxtaposed amidst the musty smell, created by years of enthusiastic fingering through knowledge. Due to the amount of artefacts on display, the knowledge started to blur and my concentration wandered. At random, like a scene from the Thomas Crown Affair, the excitement level was raised from chilled to considerably miffed by the alleged action of a group of lads, an 18th century piano and a scratch. Security guards everywhere, a state of high alert and for once I wasn't responsible!

The Van Gogh Museum is only a short walk or even shorter pedal ride from the Rijksmuseum. Everybody knows Van Gogh, but do they really understand the person and his constant struggles with depression and psychiatric issues? Well this is clearly the place to learn all about the great man. It is home to a impressive collection of his paintings, drawings and letters which paint a vivid picture of his life and work. Top works on display include, Sunflowers, The Bedroom, The Yellow House and a unique selection of self-portraits, all housed in provocative modern and contemporary surroundings

The city comes alive at night; it takes on a very different personality. That evening we explored the fascinations of the Red Light District. What an adventure, not so much seedy, but an uncomfortable atmosphere followed us as we wandered through the bustling streets. The air clogged with a heady mix of testosterone and cannabis, like a surreal Bisto trail. The interactions were good natured and at no stage did we feel unsafe or in any danger.

The next morning I pedalled to the nearby floating flower market on the banks of the Singel and then onto Anne Frank's Huis. The weather was again behaving with the traffic not as compliant. The floating flower market was splashed with early morning sunshine and is believed to be the only one if its kind in the world. The small shops are located inside a row of floating barges – a holdover from the days when flowers arrived in Amsterdam every day from the countryside by boat. The aromas overwhelmed my senses, the colours were arousing. On display were plenty of fresh bunches; as expected, tulips prevailed but there was also a mix of bulbs and seeds (including cannabis). The bulbs were ready for export, so you could enjoy them at home too. In December the market also sells the ubiquitous Christmas tree and a large selection of festive decorations.

I continued onwards, negotiating the busy and tricky Dam Square enroute to the most famous canal house in the City. It's a perfect location to people watch, but pricey. Several tram lines traverse and converge in the city's main square with passengers boarding and alighting like a human conveyor belt. After weaving through the masses, I arrived outside the notably modern façade of Anne Frank's Huis. For more than two years Anne and her family lived in the annex of the building at Prinsengracht 263 where Anne's father, Otto Frank, also had his business. It was strange and emotional to walk through the doorway to the annex that was concealed behind a moveable bookcase constructed especially for this purpose. On August 4, 1944, the hiding place was betrayed. The people in hiding were deported to various concentration camps. Only Otto Frank survived the war and arranged for Anne's inspirational words to be published as a book. Nowadays, the rooms within the property, though empty, still breathe the atmosphere of that period of time, imperceptibly eerie. Quotations from the diary, historical documents, photographs, film images, and original objects that belonged to those in hiding and the helpers illustrate the events that took place here and allow you to contemplate the horrors of war and how it impacts on real people's lives. During her time in hiding, Anne wrote a diary, developing into a talented writer. The original diary and other notebooks are on display in the museum. The whole experience is very moving and tastefully presented. It made me so thankful for my life in relative freedom. I would highly recommend a visit especially if you want to see a different more refined and less frenetic side to the city.

My final destination of the day was the Centraal Station, the main focal and arrival point for most travellers to the city. As I approached I was astonished by the mega cycle-racks on the western side of the ornate train station. It is built in the water, in front of the Ibis hotel. The Fietsflat (translates as bicycle building) was built in 2001 and can accommodate 2,500 bikes on three levels. Centraal Station is the beating heart of the city, it accommodates over 250,000 people each day and is the hub for the transport network with several tram and bus lines converging outside. The notable Neo-Renaissance façade is engaging and has been open to the public since 1889. The main tourist office is opposite housed in a traditional wooden white Dutch house. It is open daily between nine a.m. – six p.m. and is where you can purchase the iAmsterdam card, as well as offering a wide variety of services (especially city maps).

Amsterdam is the one place on the planet where fear-mongering about cycling is non-existent and it shows. With the city ruled by bikes and a self-confident assurance from the riders, instrumental in this laidback attitude is the widespread thirty km/h zones and the tight narrow streets which can only create a slowing of the traffic. There are few places where I have enjoyed urban cycling as much as in Amsterdam, I challenge anybody to stand on the corner of any busy intersection and not see a bike or bikes, they are absolutely everywhere. The City's definite major attraction is its individuality.

The vision for the future of Amsterdam is perfectly highlighted by Michel Post from the Fietserbonds (the Dutch Cyclists' Union that campaigns for better cycling conditions in the Netherlands). The city's car traffic will decrease to the point where there won't be a need for cycle lanes at all, as bicycles move off the curb and claim the streets. "Cars will consider themselves guests," he says, elevating Amsterdam's status as the world's biking Capital to new heights.

BMX, the craze is as popular as ever (August 2014)

I had organised an outing to the British BMX series eight & nine in Birmingham and had to accept I was going to be completely out of my comfort zone. The BMX phenomenon of the 1970s and 1980s passed me by, my concentration was elsewhere, which I regret. As I grew up, my chosen ride was the lumpy, hefty and not so charismatic, Grifter. In hindsight the BMX (or Bicycle Motorcross) with its compact size and manoeuvrability would have provided a much better and trendy option. The BMX story began in the early '70s when children would race their bikes care-free on dirt tracks throughout southern California. By 1977 the American Bicycle Association (ABA) was created as a national sanctioning body, and it never looked back.

The first World Championships took place in 1982, and, in 2003, the International Olympic Committee made BMX racing a full medal Olympic sport. It had finally made it, rightly recognised across the globe. So on a balmy, wet summer's day I was here at the Birmingham BMX track in Perry Barr to discover what all the fuss was about, and hopefully be converted to the highly technical, exciting and tactical sport of BMX racing. The event is held over the whole weekend, with series eight being held on the Saturday and series nine on the Sunday. I had arrived mid-morning, and the early part of the day was allocated to practice laps with the competition usually commencing around midday.

The craze is everywhere in the UK, with tracks springing up all over the country at a rapid rate. Its appeal to the masses is indisputable; it's relatively cheap in comparison to the other forms of cycle sport and sells itself effectively as a family affair with categories for all ages. The bikes consist of a single gear and usually just a simple rear brake. A standard bike will have twenty inch wheels but smaller sizes are used by the junior riders. There is also a larger twenty-four inch wheel cruiser class, which is popular with larger or older riders. As with most pastimes, entry level bikes are reasonably priced, but a top-class machine can be very expensive with a mass of gadgets.

I thought I would do a bit of homework before the day with the hope of limiting my embarrassing ignorance to all things BMX. I set about scanning the British Cycling website for a list of the current standings going into the event in Birmingham. The plan was simple; I would throw a familiar name into the conversation if I felt my knowledge was in question. Unfortunately what I discovered wasn't just a list, it was an encyclopaedia of BMX data, a blur of age groups, names, clubs and a jumble of numbers in tabular form. This was really serious stuff. As I flicked I recognised a team, the 'Redditch Premiers BMX Club'; my cousin Benn has had a long standing relationship with this club, so I decided it would be wholly appropriate to lend them my support on the day, they didn't know how lucky (or unlucky) they were.

If my involvement of the car park was a taster, then I was in for a chaos fuelled day of excitement. The place was heaving with colours, bikes, riders, spectators and vans blazoned with all manner of logos and funky artwork. Once inside I was astonished by the size of the place, the purpose built track a feast to my eyes with its array of concertinaed jumps, and a lofty starting ramp.

I had arranged to meet my very own guru (Benn) whose expertise would be invaluable, providing an idiots guide to the whole BMX scene. Oh and not forgetting my Uncle Brian, who has been around the scene for many years amassing a myriad of useful and useless facts. In the car journey over, my Uncle explained the days hectic schedule would begin with qualifying heats, called 'Moto's', with up to eight riders contesting, each one followed by a constant stream of knockout rounds before reaching the final which decides the overall winner. He also enthused about the sport's popularity, (I think he used the word 'Massive') when describing the constant events taking place across the UK, regional race leagues, national BMX Championships and today's event, the British Cycling's British BMX series. As the craze has evolved, it has also created, out of necessity, its own unique lingo, and to minimise any possible embarrassment, they both would also act as my personal human BMXionary…

The days itinerary of races was relentless, each race lasted under a minute. Even the appalling weather couldn't dampen the enthusiasm. The rain was now incessant, making the track extremely wet, which supposedly reduced the speed of the races. Not that I noticed with the competitors' blur of colour, demonstrating a poetic prowess as they negotiated the tricky track design with an accomplished ease. As one race concluded another followed in quick succession, the whole event organised efficiently and professionally, ensuring a tremendous fun packed day was had by riders and spectators alike.

As the event progressed the rate of races increased, a constant fervour and anticipation became evident, and this was transferred to the track. The concentration and commitment was visible on every riders face as they waited patiently in the start gates. The crowds' excitement rose, dictated by beaming smiles and noise as they awaited the gate to drop. A bizarre release of emotions occurred once the race had begun, anticipation and captivation mixed with a childlike excitement (and that was just from me, a spectator). The pace was intense, the strength and tactical ability of the riders was amazing, they exuded a quiet confidence whilst whizzing uncontrollably around the track, up and over jumps, breezing through banked corners and then in no time at all, it was over! My adrenalin was pumping so I can't imagine what emotions the riders would be experiencing. The ferocious enthusiasm of the announcer on the loud speaker only added to the overall experience, as he blurted out the name or number of each sporadic rider.

Once the Moto's had finished, there was a brief halt to proceedings before the quarter finals started. The weather was now behaving, so we had a wander around the site. Mixed between the commercial outlets selling refreshments and cycling accessories was the occasional up-turned bike with a mechanic (who was probably a dad) tinkering with the crank shaft or pedals, hoping to find that split second of speed to push their loved ones across the line in first place. As we left, the quarter finals had just finished, but there was still several hours of competition left to play out. Unfortunately for the race-goers, the sky was reigned by a collection of angry grey clouds; a downpour was a depressing certainty.

On reflection, I was exposed to an explosive, fun packed family spectacle of cycling. The compact nature of the track made for a real welcoming arena and it's usually free to spectate, with only the bigger events charging an entry fee. I will surely be returning and why not join me, it might even pique your interest enough to ride in the next event.

Sent to Coventry
(June 2014)

Any ride is a good ride in my book, I love the simplicity of exploration on two wheels, regardless of the weather. With this in mind I had a plan for a journey of contrasts, to pedal from my home town of Royal Leamington Spa (the prefix only used cynically when trying to impress and its suffix added due to the once medicinal qualities of the water) to the misunderstood and unquestionably less genteel city of Coventry.

I set off from Leamington's War Memorial, a mesmeric bronze figure with head bowed in mournful pose, but juxtaposed dissonantly amongst a glut of estate agents. It stands proudly, its presence so impressive, freely provoking thought and remembrance. Today the clarity of the light emphasised the handsome bronze life sized figure.

My route took me out onto the busy Kenilworth Road (A452) before I reverted to the blissfully tranquil roads around the Royal Agricultural Centre at Stoneleigh. The weather was behaving, the sky was overcast but thankfully the predicted wind and rain had failed to arrive. Considering I had only just left the urban sprawl, the calm that descended was so contrasting.

The descent into the quaint village of Stoneleigh was exhilarating, the hill was completely enveloped in dazzling greenery which only heightened my senses and focus. The speedy downhill had tested my concentration levels because I could feel my tongue protruding from my mouth, a common sign of deep thought in the Whitlock family (I admit it doesn't happen that often). I breezed over the river before exposing my nostrils to the pungent aroma of the nearby sewage works.

Why Coventry? The simple answer is: why not? I do have a modicum of sympathy towards the City and its people, it has many harsh critics and, to many, it conjures thoughts of an unprepossessing place that has suffered years of post-industrial decline. Unfortunately, it's best known for its inclusion in the British idiom 'to send someone to Coventry', the process of ostracising by non-communication or simple alienation. It's the favourite weapon of childish bullies across the globe, and its actual origins are unknown, but it is believed that events in and around Coventry during the English Civil War may have a bearing. On the positive, it is also home to Jaguar Land Rover and is where the two tone pop phenomenon started in the late '70s.

But, as the Specials sang on two tone all those years ago, it is a "concrete jungle". The first real indication I had hit the city was the emergence of bland underpasses and subways, the ever present of any urbanised metropolis. Thankfully the city is easy to navigate by bike, offering plenty of designated cycle paths and the ubiquitous on road cycle lanes, you will undoubtedly encounter a multitude of one way systems. Vigilance and common sense (an under-rated facet nowadays) is essential at all times.

If I am being truthful the City has suffered a decline in recent times (mirrored by the football team); stark evidence of this is in its buildings which are comparatively young, especially in and around the heart of the city. They could benefit from a productive makeover. The grey drab façades create a rather melancholy air (it would never be described as being crammed with disturbingly expensive designer shops, more working class, than pretentious indulgence) but it does offer several teasing hidden gems. The city is being reborn, its resolute and strong character has created a resurgence in fortunes, and this is what I hoped to find from the saddle. My initial destination was the city's historic flagship attraction, the Cathedral.

As I approached the building I was taken aback by the imposing figure of Sir Jacob Epstein's bronze sculpture of St Michael standing over the devil, the figure possesses an overwhelming power, a simple statement of divine presence with arms flung wide to welcome all. On the night of 14 November 1940 the city changed forever following some expertly executed bombing raids by the Luftwaffe. The 14th Century Cathedral was hit several times and it burned with a large part of the city. The old quarter, with its collection of black and white timber domiciles, was one of the most notably devastated areas. The ruined shell that remains is a fetching example of fortitude through devastation at the hands of humanity. A truly magical interplay of spirited art, religion and kinship. The new structure designed by Sir Basil Spence is magnificently simple, the modern wide open expanse of the nave is oddly comforting. I sat, immersed in the sobering silence. Only the tower, spire, outer wall and the bronze effigy and tomb of its first bishop survived. Shortly after the bombing two of the charred medieval roof timbers were discovered fallen in the shape of a cross. They were set dramatically in the ruins, more recently another cross was fashioned from three medieval nails by a local priest, this is referred to somewhat appropriately as the Cross of Nails and is recognised as the sign of defiance, faith and simple hope..

As I left, I caught a whimsical image of the Holy Trinity Church, I was intrigued. Its location awkwardly sandwiched between Wetherspoons and a string of high street stores. The church's simple and subdued exterior doesn't prepare you for the absolutely enthralling interior, the stained glass windows are breathtaking. The mystical stillness provides a pleasant setting to visually explore the infamous 'Doom painting', known by many as the 'Apocalypse painting'. It's extraordinary to believe the simple but lifelike figures are nearly six hundred years old, their power is astonishing and demonstrate the battle of good over evil and the eternal consequences faced by many. The images so vivid, so dark, so expressive representing so aptly the ultimate choice, Salvation or damnation! I was finding it hard to contain my emotions, so I left.

After contemplating my considerably meagre existence I pedalled away from the stillness along Trinity Street. In keeping with the adage that life is a journey, my next port of call was the Transport Museum. For over 100 years Coventry has been the centre of the UK motor industry, both four and two-wheeled, associated with such illustrious names as the aforementioned Jaguar Land Rover, Daimler, Triumph, Massey Ferguson and Peugeot, so its only appropriate that it has a museum to honour the endeavours of its skilled workers over the years. Even black cabs have been sent to Coventry and are manufactured in the city by Geely.

I was immediately faced by the impressive contemporary Whittle Arch which is supposed to replicate a large double wing. It's a refreshing accompaniment to a statue of Sir Frank Whittle whose contribution to history is legendary. He is credited with inventing the turbojet engine which revolutionised air travel and was a son of the city, being born in Earlsdon in 1907. As I traipsed across the courtyard under the arch I discovered a spectacularly surreal world map beneath my feet; in one simple step for mankind, I managed to travel between Pyonyang and Beijing. If only it was that simple!

The museum is a joy, I absolutely love the place, a jumble of cars, buses, motorbikes and a whole section dedicated to the humble bicycle, lie within. Its extensive collection of vehicles is acknowledged as being one of the finest in the world, and it offers a fantastic day out for all the family, as well as providing a perfect snapshot of the city's motoring past. Parts of the museum have been recreated to allow the visitor to face the atmosphere of the Blitz. The dark, dank surroundings provide a brief insight into what the people of the city had to endure and is testament to the strength and determination of the populace. The majority of my many visits always involve me speeding through the motor vehicles section before spending an unhealthy length of time exploring the cycling section and its dizzying array of bikes. (I feel no need to detail in words my nerdy excitement). Before departing I stopped in the foyer for a reasonably priced coffee, and watched the frenetic movements from the bus station.

Nothing stays still in Coventry for long.

The Dutch Press Awards, the prestigious event at the Residence of the Dutch Ambassador in London (March 2015)

I was surprised and proud in equal measures to be personally invited to this most prestigious event in the heart of our capital. The previous year I had written a simple but passionate article on Amsterdam and the many attractions on offer to the humble cyclist. My visit was one of complete adoration and I left feeling overwhelmed and happy in my heart to count the city as one of the friendliest, pragmatic and aesthetically captivating anyone, whether a cyclist or a simple tourist can encounter anywhere on our handsome planet. That's got to be worth a nomination at next year's event, I jest! The following paragraph from my Amsterdam piece perfectly sums up why the city is adored by many. 'The city's architecture is influenced by gables, in spout, step, neck and bell styles. The opulent houses which enjoy memorable vistas of the canals impress not so much with their size but with their overall distinguishing features and character. The vibrant colours and welcoming facades of these predominately private dwellings gives Amsterdam a wealth of architectural marvels unsurpassable by no other city in Europe. I love taking photographs; they provide a unique portal to understand a place. What we often don't see initially becomes clear when you take the time to look and linger. The vivid colours of a building, the mundane enhanced by a simple action, the understated beauty of a fleeting moment of reality. Amsterdam's cityscape is the ideal canvas, full of visual clichés providing a contemporary mixture of chaotic movement and relaxing stillness provided by the bike, the water and the sun shaded back streets'. I think that says it all!

I was genuinely shocked to have received an invite and clearly I would response positively, who wouldn't? Holland or the Netherlands is becoming a regular gig for me as I am making another appearance on its shores in April. On this occasion Utrecht is the destination, undeniably the Tour de France is my selfish draw (the city is the venue for the 2015 Grand Depart) but I am looking forward to immerse in the culture and gastronomy of the area. The Dutch are extremely proud to be hosting the Grand Depart and will no doubt provide a fitting departure for this prestigious sporting event. This is fate, the greatest cycling nation, hosting the greatest cycling, arguably sporting, event in the world.

The venue for the awards evening was the Dutch Ambassadors residence, once the doors opened I was exposed to another world, all shiny and well presented, even the staff were wearing shiny smiles. The exquisite décor of the entrance hall as I ventured up a level was furnished with all manner of historical artefacts. I was greeted by a mass of well presented people, the majority writers and the Deputy Ambassador who I later established was a keen cyclist who enthusiastically offered to write some material for me, although I'm not sure if she was just being polite, albeit she did seem genuinely interested.

As the evening progressed, the wine flowed and the constant stream of delicious canapés kept all happy whilst the conversation was constant. Most engrossed in animated discussion about the Netherlands and its many delights and attractions, at times it felt the attendees had forgotten why they were actually present, the chat was that intriguing.

Eventually we were all reminded of the exact reason as the smartly dressed individuals (and I!) were called to assemble in the main living area, the ceremony had begun. The awards were distributed in an informal fashion and all the winners appeared pleasantly surprised to receive the modern and stylish awards. Once the formalities were over, there was plenty of more time to carry on where we had left off. The conversation was still as interesting but maybe more raucous as the alcohol continued to flow. The evening ended with the Deputy Ambassador desperate for me to see her bike which was chained to a lamp-post outside. She was evidentially proud that she cycled the city streets of the capital and I commend her for her allegiance to her nation, and its fascination and total commitment to all things two wheeled.

I sincerely hope I receive an invite next year, I would miss the intelligent, vivacious and amusing conversations and the warm and hospitable welcome. Oh not forgetting the DFDS Seaways cupcake which was a surprising hit!

Team Wiggle Honda in Ghent, or was it? (February 2015)

What can I say to convince you it's an arduous existence being an editor of a successful cycling magazine. The stresses of endless deadlines, problems with content or crappy images and the constant headache of proofing and more proofing (thank you my ever patient long suffering and committed wife). Although, don't let me deceive you into thinking it's all misery, despair and long hours. There are some benefits…

So when I stumbled on an email mid morning one boring unmemorable weekday I was pleasantly surprised, in fact that was an understatement. The email was lengthy but what stood out in vivid black and white was 'Meet and interview Team Wiggle Honda in Belgium'. I replied positively and immediately, who wouldn't? I had followed the team from afar since their creation in 2013 with the help of the Bradley Wiggins Foundation and British Cycling. My interest easily peaked at the Prudential RideLondon Elite Women's race as I stood on the finish line and watched Giorgia Bronzini display her power to pip Olympic Champion Marianne Vos on the line, with Lizzie Armitstead a close third. I admired and still admire the young talent that they possess, and nurture, to ultimate success and a main factor in that winning attitude is the Team Principal, the not so shy Rochelle Gilmore. The Aussie had an illustrious career in the saddle and she is now successfully imparting her knowledge and determination so efficiently and expertly. They are unequivocally going places with their individual skill, flair and all round cycling ability, but that was always going to be the case with Gilmore at the helm.

As always with these things the itinerary was hectic, bordering on chaos, but hey that's why we do this, to push ourselves to understand life and interact with those individuals that provide enjoyment and focus for many people. A few days before departure my mind was pre-occupied with my interviewing style, I had decided on a mix of Jeremy Paxman and Ali G. Acting like an idiot would come easy but the forceful, predatory manner of Mr Paxman was just not in my psyche, well that was the hope.

Unfortunately all this preparation was to go to waste as I was to miss the trip due to illness, but I feel the exceptional qualities and characters of the team are still totally worthy of some page space.

The team was to be unveiled in Ghent, Belgium, it would be their first time together as a complete team to train and prepare for the 2015 season. Although this was the first official assembly of the team members, the riders had already enjoyed success in 2015. In January, Chloe Hosking scored the team's first win of the season by taking Stage 1 of the Bay Classic Series, and then went on to come second overall in the Tour of Qatar where Wiggle Honda won the teams classification. Peta Mullens also won the Australian National Championships in January and Jolien D'hoore was successful in the Belgium National Omnium Championships. Giorgia Bronzini had continued her good form from 2014 and had taken stage wins in both the Bay Cycling Classic and the Tour Down Under, with Annette Edmondson finishing the Tour Down Under with the Green Sprinters Journey. So the signs were very good for the 2015 season.

Wiggle Honda has a diverse mix of nationalities, with team members representing nine nations, and based in Belgium. According to team Managing Director Rochelle Gilmore "The 2015 season has got off to an exciting start and this is the result of an intensive team focus on performance and results. Currently ranked third on the UCI rankings, we believe that this season we can reach a completely new level, with the quality of our riders combined with the expertise and experience of the support team. Potentially we can win the Giro, Grand Tours and also, the Classic style races. Each victory we record helps build our team spirit."

Adam Ryan, Head of Brand Marketing at Wiggle, the team's main sponsor and the World's biggest online cycling and trisports retailer, says. "Wiggle is proud to sponsor Wiggle Honda and is really excited by the team's potential for success this year, as well as its potential to help grow the awareness and support of Women's professional cycling. Wiggle's relationship with the team is a vital part of our on-going commitment to getting more women cycling, a commitment that we know is enthusiastically shared by Wiggle Honda and these incredible athletes".

It offers so much more than 1066! (August 2014)

It was that time of year again, August had arrived much quicker than expected. The heavenly sunshine of June and July a distant memory, replaced with gloomy drizzle and below average temperatures, ideal weather for our annual camping adventure. Our destination was East Sussex, on the border with Kent. The campsite was situated on the outskirts of the small village of Staplecross in the heart of the Wealds, with its charming historic hop houses dotting the landscape. We were central to most things, Hastings was only eight miles, Rye ten miles and Battle six miles. The surroundings enclosed by undulating rustic roads and plenty of thriving greenery (thanks to the August rain!).

After several days ignoring the bike, I was itching to get out on two wheels. As I poked my head tentatively from beneath the canvas, I was dismayed by the weather. The sky monopolised by a depressing grey gloom and the temperature was on the chilly side. After a short pedal my gloveless hands were already numb, the weather in Barcelona in January was significantly warmer in comparison. What had happened to the splendid summer? I pondered as I pedalled towards Staplecross. The hub of the village is most undoubtedly the local convenience store, which is well stocked and agreeable. I breezed past this morning, the place was already bustling with the locals on the hunt for a daily newspaper or piping hot pastry.

I had decided to pedal to Robertsbridge, I followed the B2089 towards Cripps Corner, the surroundings governed by arable farmland and the greenery of dense woodland, it was easy to feel part of nature when I stumbled on Brede High Woods which is situated off the B2089. The wood consists of 647 acres of ancient and secondary woodland which is home to a diverse array of wildlife. It's known for its invertebrates, in particular the Flea Beetle (Longitarus Longiesta) and Glow Worms. This morning the setting was eclipsed by tranquillity, the broadleaved woodland was so peaceful as I entered through the Broad Oak Brede Road car park. The Woodland Trust acquired the site in 2007 and have committed to protecting and improving the habitat for biodiversity and improving access to the public. I found a sunny spot on the outskirts of the greenery and sat for sometime, just me, the bike and the silence. My only company was an engaging array of woodland butterflies and the occasional repertoire from the local birdlife.

I pedalled on, my focus Robertsbridge, I negotiated the busy A21 north and after a gradual climb I arrived on the High Street in this quaint village. Many of the oldest existing houses date back to the 14th and 15th century, one of the finest is the Seven Stars public house and several with vivacious blooms spilling from window ledges, scenting the air. I propped my bike up near the distinctive War Memorial clock tower and went off to explore. The village manages to maintain that timeless appeal even with the usual modern intrusions and I was interested to read that it is in fact home to the Gray-Nicholls company which began making cricket bats in 1876. It was like travelling back in time.

My next destination was Battle, the route along the A21 and then the A2100 slalomed its way mostly downhill. At St Johns Cross I had to follow the A2100 and the majority of the route was completely ruled by tree cover, the greenery creating a natural tunnel before I emerged into bright sunlight and the outskirts of Battle. The attractive town is famous for its association with the Battle of Hastings and is captivated by the interesting Abbey of St Martin set imposingly amongst a glut of high street shops, restaurants and cafés. The colour of the stonework was hypnotic as the sun danced off its elegant façade. There is no disputing the splendour of its construction.

It is hard to imagine that this quiet market town witnessed probably the most important and memorable battle to take place on English soil. It's even claimed that within the grounds of the Abbey is the exact spot where King Harold is said to have died. The Abbey was constructed following the battle between 1070 and 1094 and a thriving community was created. There is plenty to do for all the family with a highlight being the battlefield (re-living the battle through the media of a free audio-guide) and the chance to explore the well preserved ruins of the original Abbey. I especially enjoyed the Abbey walls with their unsurpassed views of the town and the tantalising prospect of spying on the locals.

From Battle I continued south towards the holiday resort of Hastings, the ride maintained a downhill momentum, and I breezed effortlessly into the confines of this attractive town. My destination was the seafront, chiefly the 'Net Shops' which are basically tall wooden sheds unique to Hastings used to store all manner of fishing gear. These unusual structures were created in the Victorian era to counter the lack of space when the sea came much closer to the cliffs and land was limited, so they ingeniously built up instead of out. I negotiated the main commercial part of the town with ease and halted in front of Pete's Eastern Fish shop. The aromas of the sea gripped my senses, firing my imagination.There are plenty of outlets on offer to buy fresh locally caught fish, all busy distributing the catch of the day. I wandered happily around this timeless setting, the surroundings engrossed by the tall and narrow Net Shops with the odd boat or anchor nestled nonchalantly, almost everywhere you look there is something of its rich seafaring history. After pausing briefly by the entrance to the funicular Cliff Railway which was opened in 1903 and originally operated on the water balance principle before being modernised in the '70s and converted to electric, I set off back towards the family.

I retraced my way back up the A2100 and through Battle, the tree cover now frivolously eerie with the occasional pocket of sunlight penetrating the darkness, the landscape slowing, closing in, the journey was more arduous due to the gradual incline. My final stop of day was to be the small village of Bodiam which was conveniently on my route back to the campsite. Bodiam has two major attractions, the Kent and East Sussex Railway and Bodiam Castle. After negotiating several rapid descents and more trees, I arrived in front of the brightly coloured gates of the steam railway. The line gently makes it way from Bodiam to Tenterden, described as the 'The Jewel of The Weald' for ten and half miles through the mesmerising countryside of the Rother Valley. I pedalled the short distance along the quiet country lanes to the entrance of the castle grounds.

The castle is captivating, the setting is so picturesque, set in the heart of open countryside. The 14th century structure is consumed by defined battlements and a formidable portcullis. Its appearance is enhanced by the tranquil waters of the moat overlooked by a plethora of narrow windows used as lookouts or to fire arrows at unwanted guests. It's even believed the site would have been elaborately landscaped with ponds and pools. A tourist treat today but in the past, it was essential for defence. Unfortunately the building became unliveable during the English Civil War and fell into disrepair. It was restored predominately with the help of Lord Curzon, Viceroy of India. The grounds offer an abundance of places to sit and relax and I easily imagined coming face-to-face with knights and courtiers in these sublime surroundings.

The next day, I had hatched a noticeably unconventional and risky plan. I had suggested to the clan that we should ride as a family unit (including the dog) along the seafront in Hastings. The only issue we encountered was locating a bike with a basket big enough to accommodate the dog. Eventually, we hired bikes from two separate outlets, Bells Bikes provided a wide selection of vintage bikes and city bikes (and plenty of baskets) and was conveniently located just off the promenade, in the Old Town. The setting bewitching with its collection of narrow streets and twittens (alleys) used over the centuries by smugglers and now home to a plethora of antique shops, atmospheric pubs, restaurants and the odd traditional sweet shop which pre-occupied the children. Unfortunately they could not facilitate the two younger members of our group, Eli and Lauren. So we made our way back to the seafront and hired some more appropriate transportation from the Hastings Seafront cycle hire.

We set off from the 'Stade' meaning 'Landing Place' in old Saxon which is home to Europe's largest beach launched fishing fleet. Our route was to Bexhill and we were following the promenade, the weather was warm with a slight westerly breeze. The far-reaching views of the sea on our left were majestic, the odd crescendo of white water crashing on the sand was spine-tingling. The route was in relatively good condition with a mix of Tarmac and gravel.

The ancient coastline was established over 138 million years ago in the Cretaceous period when it was a subtropical flood plain. It was a joy to pedal so close to the sea, the cycle path was relatively quiet and mirrored the pedestrian path. As a collective we were maintaining a good pace, the kids happily weaving through the occasional pedestrian as they encroached onto the dedicated cycle path. The dog appeared happy sat cocooned in the wicker basket, his focus and concentration in front transfixed on the kids and the cinematic views, promoting images of Snoopy in aviator googles.

Unfortunately, his focus was too concentrated as he made several attempts to leap like a salmon in a bid to join the group of young cyclists picking up speed on the horizon. In a bid to prevent the envisioned carnage it was agreed we would pedal on more aware of maintaining a greater semblance of a collective unit. As we approached Galley Hill I remembered I had read about a submerged forest off the shoreline, which is partly visible when the tide is out, four thousand year old tree stumps mark its location. After a much needed rest we encountered a brief but testing climb up Galley Hill, the highest spot along this stretch of coastline. The views were simply extraordinary in all directions and in the late 1700s a 'Signal Station' was built as a chain of lookouts.

We only made the outskirts of Bexhill and after a fast food lunch stop we retraced our route with the wind on our backs. We even managed to create our own mini peloton, with each rider sub-consciously taking over the lead. The noise was one of happy chatter mixed with occasional banter and in relatively no time we found ourselves back on the promenade in Hastings, all enthusiastic and desperate to repeat the small adventure again in the future. I can't be sure that Wilf, our sausage dog, had the same opinion, as he forlornly waddled off, unsure what he had witnessed over the past few hours.

Ballyhoura, the provocative mountains in and around Limerick (February 2015)

We were travelling again. This time our destination was the Ballyhoura Mountains in Co. Limerick. We had flown to Cork and, after a short winding drive, we negotiated the pleasant town of Mitchelstown, just off the M8 (the main motorway linking Cork with Dublin). We then took the R513 in the direction of Kilfinnane. After several detours and phone calls we eventually arrived in the town and our base for the weekend. The town is moderate in size but, like with most provincial towns in Ireland, it was full of pubs. It's situated in the Southwest of Ireland, strategically on the borders of the counties of Limerick, Tipperary and Cork. The attractive town has remains of a 14th Century Castle and the present day town was laid out in the 18th Century with the simple but exquisite church being built in 1878.

We had been kindly invited to stay at the Ballyhoura Hostel, which had recently been renovated by the owner Seamus Nunan. The house was previously his family home and it was great to hear his interesting stories of his childhood, he is passionate about his hometown after returning from Dublin and has spent a lot of money and sweat on making the hostel a charming place to be. The Hostel is described as 'five star hostelling' and seamlessly combines the comfort of a top hotel with the freedom and value of a hostel stay, it's a genius concept and one that unquestionably works, especially with its close proximity to the Ballyhoura Mountains and the plethora of outdoor activities on offer. The décor is compelled by the outdoors both visually and aromatically. The senses are treated to the enchantment of many forms of wood; Seamus is a carpenter by trade and his skill is evident in the quantity of striking furniture and fixtures that are tastefully dotted throughout the property. The dining area is bewitched by decoratively sculptured stools using recycled tree stumps, but I was captivated by the selection of tables which again had been created from the same stumps, their appearance just compels you to touch and caress the intricate composition.

Ballyhoura is a fascinating area of undulating green areas, woodland and moss laden trees set in breathtaking scenic hills and mountains. The snow-capped Galty Mountains was our ever-present, and impressive, companion. The Mountain Bike trails are nestled in some magnificent surroundings, designed by Daffyd Davis and run over ninety kilometres of the most stunning undulating hills and forests that Ireland has to offer. The trail system was created over seven years ago in Coilltes Greenwood Forest and hosted the European Marathon MTB Championship in June 2014. It consists of narrow single-track and boardwalk sections and also has tantalising stretches of forest road climbs over both short and long distances. The trails are laid out in five loops and each loop leads onto the next. The loops are well signed with frequent colourful way markers in one direction – just pick the colour of the loop you want to ride and follow the arrows, it's as simple as that. Facilities at the trail head include map boards, car parking, toilets, showers and bike wash facilities. Trail friendly accommodation, bike rental and good food are available locally.

Before commencing our dirty adventure we had a chat with the animated and passionate Chris O'Callaghan from the Trailriders Bike

Hire Centre. He explained that the trails are constantly busy and this was proven by the cavalcade of cyclists heading towards the start point. He suggested we try the Green Loop which he explained would offer easy climbs and fun single-track descents and is the shortest of all the loops but would ultimately give us a flavour of the Ballyhoura Trails. It is essentially one gradual climb followed by one long descent with all but 1.5 km of the loop on narrow, twisty single-track trails. It sounded ideal!

Sarah and I were given two lightweight full suspension models (hers a Cube and mine a BMC) and we set off from the well-stocked shop. The weather was fair and warm, with, thankfully, no sign of the gales that had greeted us from our slumber. We had decided on the green loop as Chris praised its qualities and also because of Sarah's limited mountain biking expertise. The Greenwood Loop is the first of five loops in the trail system and takes you through the lush hillsides underneath Seefin Mountain and Black Rock and is used as the outward and inward legs for the rest of the trail network. The trail was initially steep as we progressed slowly up the mountain, the track was well maintained with the occasional boulder to keep our concentration. Our tyres groaned against the dirt and debris, our brakes creaked as we made good progress. I love this time of year, the landscape turning from browns and the desolation of winter to the beginning of greens and zesty colours of spring. The middle section was relatively benign as we pedalled into the shadows of the tree cover. There was a March chill in the air but the sun was already generating a pleasurable warmth. Sarah was coping like an expert; her initial apprehension had diminished and she was leaning into the corners (I thought at one stage she was going to attempt a Rocky Drop Off!), appearing to be enthused even as her appearance became increasingly mud-splattered.

After stopping briefly, we emerged on a crude Tarmac section with staggering far-reaching views of the surrounding hillside. Galvanised we then hit more tree cover creating a natural tunnel with the occasional chink of light guiding our way. Due to the recent wet weather the trails were slippery particularly in the more shaded areas and on occasions can be tolerably narrow (not more than 1m wide) but that just adds to the all-round fun.

We crossed a fast flowing stream before climbing again, eventually reverting to a rutted grass track at the crest of a hill. At this stage I was rather worried about Sarah's abilities as the trails became quite technical in places, featuring some elevated timber boardwalk sections with exposed edges, but she performed like a pro.

The complete scene of isolation was astonishing, the surface was still okay. It was satisfying to see a mix of all ages and sizes throwing themselves down the mud laden trails: fathers and sons, middle-aged mildly rotund blokes, and athletic teenagers. The only common factors were the continual smiling faces and the dirt splattered bikes and clothing.

From the point the well-defined track contoured downwards, the views were breathtaking, a backdrop embroidered in green hues with a smattering of stone dwellings and snow-capped mountains. The surface was now variable including a quantity of loose rocks, gravel, mud, deep cavernous puddles and protruding roots but it didn't prevent us pedalling at a relatively fast pace. What followed was a thrilling descent on a bumpy, muddy track and with some heavy braking we arrived safely at the still-busy carpark. On reflection we both had so much fun, but me probably more than Sarah. The set up at Ballyhoura is masterful; the people as always in Ireland, were unbelievably convivial and accommodating. The welcome from Seamus and Theresa at the hostel was so genuinely hospitable; we truly felt part of their extended family. The strap line on their literature states “You won’t want to leave” and it is so true. We will be returning in the future, that’s a definite.

I would like to briefly mention Blarney Castle which we detoured to, en route back to Cork Airport. We all know of the Castle and the believed powers of the famous stone (the gift of eloquence) but the castle itself is a magnificent example of fortification and its dramatic imposing structure is recognised as one of Ireland’s finest historical buildings. The stone is set in the wall of the battlements and to kiss it, you have to demonstrate some gymnastic prowess by leaning backwards (holding onto the iron railings) from the parapet walk, whilst being held by a member of staff (who, in my case, was a substantially frail chap, not dis-similar to Mr Burns from Simpsons fame).

An unpredicted outcome in the Aveyron (November 2014)

I had been invited to the South of France in the middle of November and the weather was going to be unpredictably changeable, just like the UK. The trip had been organised by the obliging people at Freewheel Holidays, a Leicester based company who specialise in cycling holidays for groups, families, first timers and keen cyclists who just want to simply discover Europe from the saddle.

The BA flight from Heathrow to Toulouse was on a damp slight dreary morning, I was hoping for some improvement at my destination, fingers crossed. The flight was comfortable and relatively short and I arrived on time in Toulouse. As I waited in the arrivals lounge for Claudia, who would be my host for the next couple of days, I noticed the weather through the terminal windows; wet and gloomy was the best description. Over the short drive to Plaisance, we discussed cycling and how the interest and popularity in the area has increased significantly over the past few years. The approach to Plaisance was impressive, surrounded by plenty of small attractive hamlets and villages and cocooned by oak, walnut and chestnut forests. Its appeal is enhanced by its close proximity to the unspoiled River Tarn and the World Heritage Site town of Albi.

On arrival I was shown to my room to briefly freshen up before Claudia explained in detail her plans for the next couple of days. The riding (especially the distances) was all dependent on the weather, she explained. She made a conscious effort on several occasions to reassure me that throughout the summer months the sun was ever present with uninterrupted blue skies. Even now the clarity of the light was mesmerising, the colours vivid and every contour of the striking landscapes perfectly detailed.

Les Magnolias is a luxurious twenty-two bedroom, traditional boutique hotel set in the tranquil Aveyron countryside in the ancient and enchanting village of Plaisance in the Midi-Pyrenees, South West France. Open all year round, the hotel boasts its own dedicated and popular chef, Yves Coeurveille. The seven hundred year old property was recently renovated by the owner Dietmar Ley and was once the home of famous French poet, Paul Valéry. The hotel operation is run adeptly by Claudia Ley who also manages Cycling Magnolias, a cycling operation based at the hotel, established in 2011 to encourage cyclists from all over the world to experience the idyllic cycling surroundings. She is ably assisted in the management of the hotel by Michele Coeurveille.

I couldn't wait for the following day to arrive with the tantalising prospect of exploring the rapturous surroundings on a bike. So after a sumptuous gourmet meal and the effects of an early start I fell asleep in no time cuddling the Michelin maps I had purchased before my departure.

I awoke the next morning with half of the Midi-Pyrenees stuck to my forehead, thankfully the map had not been decimated by the mass of dribble and fidgeting. After a hearty breakfast, I was more than ready to pedal, the weather was rain free, notably the sun was lively and the temperature was comfortable. We had both agreed the previous evening over dinner in the hotel that we would cheat and utilise Claudia's range of Electric Bikes. She also animatedly explained that she had devised an extensive network of routes for cyclists which immerse the rider in the numerous nearby medieval villages and towns.

The plan had been lovingly detailed by Claudia: cycle to the medieval town of Albi via Ambialet, following one of the charming cycling routes. We would have lunch in Albi centre before returning to Plaisance via Phillip Andouard cycle shop and then followed by a Gourmet dinner at Les Magnolias that evening, simple and tantalising in equal measure. On the other hand, a drastic turn of events only twenty minutes into the ride would have us both questioning the use of helmets and the unfortunate consequences of not donning the appropriate safety attire. Whilst on a gradual descent into the Tarn Valley, I lost brief concentration as I fiddled with the unfamiliar battery and the bike fell beneath me dragging me along the tarmaced road. Within a split second Claudia (who I assume had to deviate to prevent a collision) had also been unseated from her bike. Time had stopped, the peacefulness of the surroundings were eerily apparent; my immediate concern was for my companion who by this time was sat in the middle of the carriageway with blood gushing from a head wound. Claudia was dazed and her phone was shattered but thankfully a local appeared and rang for some medical assistance. The next few minutes seemed like hours as we anxiously waited, I was in shock, the realisation of what had just happened still vivid and fresh in my mind. Why hadn't we both been wearing a helmet? The cycling was no longer a priority, Claudia's well-being was paramount.

The sight of poor Claudia the next day added to my cuts and bruises is stark evidence of the benefits of protective headwear. I think we have both learnt a tough hard lesson and I can personally assure you I will have a helmet on my head without fail in the future. I would just like to say that not ONE of the over two hundred cyclists that have utilised Cycling Magnolias in the past has EVER fallen off their bikes and injured themselves on any of the roads, ascents or descents... the fact is, the roads are overwhelmingly quiet and safe, as well as ravishingly beautiful. I can personally assure you that Claudia is an extremely careful guide; maybe I need to improve my cycling abilities!

I departed with some emotion; in my short visit, which consisted of just twenty minutes pedalling, I had made some good friends who were so accepting. I will return someday not only to enjoy the perfect setting for cycling but to immerse in a great place, full of exceptional people.

Monday is cricket night
(July 2013)

Every Monday evening, throughout the summer, is cricket night for my eldest son, Noah. This provides me with a weekly opportunity to enjoy the charms of the local area by bike. Mention cricket at anytime or in any conversation and your mind is automatically drawn to an image of rain or is that just me? The sport at all levels is blighted by the wet stuff, with a propensity to decimate what to some is an essential part of village life. Noah has been a keen exponent of the game for many years and wears his whites with pride, each Monday cricket occupies ninety minutes (sometimes longer) of our time so it only felt right to utilise this time to venture out and discover the local area on two wheels.

That area is Southam, a small humdrum market town in South East Warwickshire. What I was to discover was enlightening and re-enforced the fact that I should not take places for granted, even if they appear comfortably familiar. The town was first mentioned in a charter of King Ethelred in 998 but it is believed that there was an Anglo-Saxon domain before that date and it appeared in the Doomsday book under the unfortunate salubrious name of 'Sucham', make of that what you will!

My youngest son Eli was accompanying me, his excitement was blatantly evident as I unstrapped the bikes from the car rack.

Unfortunately the sun had begun to fade, grey gloomy clouds loomed over the skyline. Rain was inevitable. Thankfully we had come prepared, a stash of sweets would keep spirits high and concentration focused. The outskirts of the town are controlled by light industrial units and its importance as a market town has become inconsequential in recent years. Modern interlopers have invaded, none more so than Codemasters, who are acknowledged as Europe's largest privately owned computer games company. Its location, residing inconspicuously on the outskirts of the town, belies the forward thinking, notably geeky, development that lies within.

Our initial route took us through a boring industrial estate, we had no real plan. although I had read about a medieval water source which intrigued me. Eli is at home on a bike, his confidence is apparent but I have on occasions had to dampen his enthusiasm and today was no exception. For a nine year old, he has a good understanding of history and culture, always appearing interested and, either genuinely or cynically, he is a very good actor! The roads were busy with plenty of speeding vehicles and a lack of intelligence and common sense from their occupants. We negotiated the racetrack of the Banbury Road before heading towards the heart of the town. The main thoroughfare was relatively quiet and we halted in the tranquil confines of the local church.

St James church sits peacefully elevated; built in the thirteenth century, it is a grade one listed building and pre-dated by a Saxon structure, believed to be of wooden construction. It's a congenial old place. The churchyard peacefulness is a pleasant contrast to the bustle of the town. The grounds are particularly attractive and its position provides some appealing views over the park and towards Leamington. The attractive exterior is infatuated by the graceful tower with its simple, naively carved stone cross. It undoubtedly possesses an inescapable romantic quality. From the church we pedalled downhill at speed, we were on the trail of the Holy Well. After breezing through a residential area we encountered the eternal headache that is a gate, annoyingly interrupting the flow of the ride. The route was well signed, in fact there were a collection of metal markers identifying several trails, Harry Green Way and The Blue Lias Rings (the latter are a collection of circular walks between Southam, Stockton, Long Itchington and Bascote). A leaflet is available online or from Southam Library and helpfully identifies historic points along the route, enhanced by illustrations by Henson Bamford, a local artist. To begin, the going was smooth and relatively fast, and we were blessed with some handsome views of the energetic countryside. The only sound was the comforting crescendo of the nearby river, the air clean and fresh. A short pedal following the well-defined track transported us to the mesmerising ancient monument.

The Holy Well is a fascinating restored grade two listed monument, and its location on the outskirts of the town in the Stowe River Valley, only adds to its intriguing and spiritual nature. It has a simple inherent beauty and was reputedly used in medieval times by the monks from nearby Stoneythorpe, as well as providing a primary water supply for the townsfolk. It's a blissfully tranquil spot, the only sound was the natural mineral spring exuberantly spurting from the mouths of the skillfully carved, expressive stone gargoyles (some believe they represent the images of sun gods). Legend dictates that the water had healing qualities and it never freezes, although I have no evidence for either. I understand the water still comes from the nearby quarry area just off the main Coventry Road and its qualities are infamous, particularly for eye problems. We both agreed it felt like we were walking in the footsteps of ghosts, its cultural and historic significance so evident but so understated, it was an excellent find. Eli enjoyed the ugly features of the carvings. (I think they reminded him of Grandma).

From the Well we continued our adventure following the now less defined track, our tyres groaned as we progressed through the placid arable farmland. I was pleasantly surprised by the quality of the surface, especially considering the wet weather we had encountered over the past month. Unfortunately we encountered several other gates which did become a logistical annoyance. As the trail slalomed its way deeper into the subdued terrain we discovered the remnants of the old weir which was built to create a pond to supply power to Stoneythorpe Mill. The original stonework was barely visible, covered in years of overgrowth. It was a nice spot to pause briefly and the vantage point did afford an absorbing view of the Dallas Burston Polo Grounds. The extensive grounds are methodically manicured and it's hard to believe that it was transformed from simple farmland in 1998. The whole site encompasses six hundred acres and includes six polo pitches, a wedding venue and a five star hotel. We explored deep into the nearby tree cover on foot, the hidden nooks were so alluring, beams of sunlight piercing through the foliage. The susurration of the rushing river crashing over the inconspicuous weir was so relaxing and provided an agreeable spot to rest. It awoke a childlike wonder, images of tree climbing and the simplicity of years gone by for me but, for Eli, this was just the naive innocence of being a nine year old.

At this point we decided we needed to retrace our route back while we could, the blur of greenery was becoming disorientating. After several impromptu errors of judgement, which resulted in unseated riders and subsequent mudded knees and grass stained bottoms, not all involving Eli, we finally made it back to a semblance of civilisation, in the guise of a gang of dogs taking their owners for a walk. As we headed up Park Lane, we could be heard animatedly and enthusiastically discussing what we had just discovered and the fun we had had through a speculative detour into the countryside. Next I felt it vital to show Eli the delectable architecture of the Manor House which is set in the heart of the town, at the intersection of several busy thoroughfares. The location contradicts its historic importance; on a positive the cashpoint opposite did allow me to check my finances. It's claimed that King Charles I stayed in the Manor House (now a pharmacy) before the Battle of Edgehill in 1642 and it is believed to be haunted, possibly by a ghostly servant girl. We stopped to marvel at the exquisite Stuart exterior, which was only discovered in 2007 when a portion of lime render fell away to reveal the simply resplendent façade. Next door is a well-stocked bike shop and the town centre offers a smattering of charming traditional shops, pubs and restaurants.

Our next destination was the sleepy village of Ladbroke, we breezed back towards the cricket club before taking the A423 signed M40 A423 Banbury. The traffic was busy, the weather had improved and we made steady progress. As we entered the outskirts of the village the faint breeze of freshly cut grass took over our senses. Ladbroke is a stereotypically sleepy English village, it has a decent pub, a spectacular eighteenth century Hall (which has now been converted into luxury living spaces) but its greatest attraction is the handsome simple church. We pedalled up to the Church of All Saints and immediately noticed a familiar sight, a strategically placed sign informed us that the Harry Green Way (a twenty-one mile circular walk, linking eight villages around Southam and devised by Harry Green, Chairman of Southam Ramblers in 1988) trailed through the churchyard. The building was originally constructed in the thirteenth century, eventually enhanced with decorated Gothic features in the fourteenth and fifteenth centuries and the bell has a ring of five bells. It provides a precious glimpse into the past. I had read that the bookmakers "Ladbrokes" was in fact named after the village. In 1886 a small credit bookmakers decided to name itself after this serene Warwickshire community and the Ladbrokes brand was created. I'm always drawn to churches and the whole ethos of remembrance and solace that is evokes. We spent sometime exploring the gravestones; they provide an insight into the local community and serve as a tool to remember individuals through the exquisite words carved in their memory. Even Eli respected the tranquil eerie surroundings briefly before unsurprisingly reverting to his somewhat boisterous self, so we left (trust me, that child could easily wake the dead).

We retraced our route back towards Southam as cricket night was coming to an end. The sun was fading and the shadows dominant, the roads were quiet and we happily pedalled, just having time to grab some sugary snacks from the local supermarket. We were both relieved that the rain had not materialised and our early return allowed us time to watch Noah handily disperse ball after ball around the field before being unceremoniously bowled out, deflecting a delivery onto his wickets. HOWZAT!

Edinburgh, a great place to honeymoon especially with a bike. (July 2014)

So as I sat on a flight up to the Scottish capital on what could only be described as a Cortina with wings (and more worryingly propeller's) I tentatively approached the topic of cycling in the city with my wife of one day, Sarah. Okay, I admit, not the most tactful of propositions, considering we were only a couple of hours into our honeymoon, but curiously she communicated a resounding thumbs up, even more reason to recognise I had made a fine choice of soulmate. This was my first visit to Edinburgh, although not Scotland, and my hope was to find a city brimming with history, culture, fine food and hopefully some fine weather.

My initial thought as we alighted the Airlink bus was 'What a City!' An assault on my eyes and ears, around every corner stood an historic sculpture or dazzling monument, all refined and captivating. We quickly located our hotel, strategically placed just off Princes Street, in the shadows of the Nelson Monument, which sits imposingly amongst the greenery of Calton Hill.

The early morning roads are tormented by buses with the sporadic cyclist dwarfed by these metal monsters. The city bustling, the noise of bagpipes, animated soft accents and those buses, they clog the thoroughfares, the congestion incessant at times. The city has an indescribable magic, it's brimming with people but somehow it maintains a noticeably rural feel, it's spectacularly surreal. Everywhere a merry face clad in tartan greets you, proudly promoting the joys of their home city. The daily reminder that you are in the capital comes in the form of the Scott Monument. It casts a domineering shadow over the commercial district of Princes Street. Yet oddly this area is in fact home to some superlative green open spaces which belie its urbanised prominence, crammed with disturbingly expensive designer shops.

The first thing to do was track down a bike, and the tourist office on Princes Street were extremely helpful in identifying several worthy contenders, as well as plying me with a bulky supply of local cycle routes. I opted for 'Cycle Scotland', located on Blackfriars Street, just off the cobblestoned Royal Mile. The owner Pete was a likeable eccentric chap with long flowing hair and an endless repertoire of animated tales about past cycle journeys and adventures. He was passionate about his trips to the Highlands and beyond. His bike hire business has been running successfully for many years, and offers both bespoke tailored cycle tours around Edinburgh, and wilderness tours of the Highlands and Islands, alongside canoe and Kayak excursions. The shop is an Aladdin's cave of bikes, Lonely Planet guides and a dizzying array of general cycling paraphernalia. My kind of placc!

We agreed that I should take a sturdy hybrid and as I departed he thrust a laminated map in my direction. He was adamant of its qualities and ensured I would have an intense experience. The map intricately detailed a route up to and around Arthur's Seat and then back towards the city following the evocatively named 'Innocent Railway cycle path'. On my way back to my hotel, I encountered plenty of cyclists, young, old, business and student types. All appeared comfortably adept at weaving in and out of the traffic, oblivious to the dangers of the constant flow of trams and buses.

I was up early the next morning, I couldn't contain my eagerness to get out and explore after Pete's enthusiasm. My route took me briefly along the unusually deserted Princes Street, passing the exquisite statue dedicated to the Duke of Wellington (which always has a seagull sat atop his head, regardless of weather or time of day) before halting briefly by the Scott Monument. Its Victorian Gothic construction is spellbinding; the tower is two hundred feet and six inches high, and has a series of viewing platforms reached by a collection of spiral staircases. The highest platform is reached by ascending two hundred and eighty-seven steps and has been eloquently described as looking like a "Gothic rocket ship". Next, I approached a slight incline as I made my way towards the Royal Mile. Again, this was relatively deserted as I headed east towards the Palace of Holyroodhouse. I paused briefly by the ornate gates to the palace, before continuing on past the parliament building and into the remoteness of Holyrood Park. The bewitching views of Margaret's Loch and the ruins of St Andrew's chapel set into the hillside were hypnotising. It was astonishing that only a few moments previous I was negotiating the urban metropolis of Scotland's capital.

What followed was a gradual but not testing climb amid a riot of birdsong and virile greenery, the occasional jogger my only company. At Dunsapie Loch the map steered me towards a path and the ascent to Arthur's Seat. I left the bike secured to a tree and continued on foot. The twisting flowing trail was in good order and after a substantial trek I arrived at Arthur's Seat, the stark beauty and panoramic views took my breath away. This is the highest point in the park and is a dormant volcano which sits 251 metres above sea level. After a lengthy rest surveying the city, I descended and continued onwards and upwards. I was following the Salisbury crags which are a series of

150ft cliff faces and again the views were superb of the city and the castle, lending its distinctive imprint to the skyline. I felt that I could reach out and touch the buildings, so captivating.

Once I had descended fully, I followed the road towards Duddington village which contoured the Loch, the sun dancing off the water. The village is a quaint place and I stopped by the gate to the Manse. Pete from the bike shop was so passionate about a secret garden hidden from the roadway behind the walls. What a find, the mystical stillness was absorbing; the only sound was me, clumsily negotiating the intricate lawns and flower beds with my cumbersome transport. Dr Neil's garden (its official title) was a mass of floral delights, shades of zippy colours and perfumes mixed seamlessly with delicate views and sounds of the neighbouring Loch. It's well worth a visit for the tranquillity and complete isolation. A genuinely compelling episode.

I reluctantly departed and was on the hunt for the 'Innocent Railway', a disused railway line which runs through the countryside back to the city. The path runs from the Newington/St Leonards area under Holyrood Park via Duddingston and Craigmillar to Brunstane in the East of the city and is part of the NCN route 1. It's believed the Edinburgh and Dalkeith Railway (opened in July 1831) earned its nickname 'the Innocent Railway' due to its safety record. It carried three hundred thousand to four hundred thousand passengers a year without any fatalities. The route took me through a wondrous green corridor, to my left was the soothing sounds of the Loch and my right was sumptuous views of Arthur's seat, the volcanic rock ignited with the bright sunlight as it caught the reflection of the sun. All perfectly complemented by an abundance of floral displays evoking a pleasant summery feeling.

I then encountered the considerably less inviting and somewhat eerie surroundings of the tunnel (Pete had informed me that they even hold parties in this disagreeable setting). The tunnel is 556 yards (518 metres) long, 20 feet (6.1 metres) wide and 15 feet (4.6 metres) high. The arched roof is lined with Craigleith stone and was completed in 1829. It was one of the earliest railways tunnels in the world. Thankfully the route was fairly well lit and I made my way tentatively through the damp interior. Eventually I appeared into some exceptional sunshine and headed towards the city centre.

As I made my way up towards the castle, I was distracted by the passionate melody of the bagpipes which appeared to resonate from every street corner. The city is easily accessible by bike or foot, and the tram service is excellent, convenient and cheap. The service runs from both the airport and the train station into the heart of the city. Cyclists are well catered for with a collection of on and off road cycle routes which are well signed and well maintained.

After following several cycle paths, I reacquainted myself with the Royal Mile enroute to Edinburgh Castle. If I am being slightly critical, the road surface in and around the Royal Mile and just off Princes Street is considerably hard work due to the presence of cobbles (just ask Sarah, later in the day I tried to give her an impromptu backie, her bum will never be the same). This area is cluttered with chic artisan boutiques and cafes. The approach to the castle is majestic as you negotiate the grandstand that hosts the Military Tattoo. The queue to buy tickets was long and laborious but the castle and its museums were adequate recompense. The laidback setting, considering the crowds, was welcoming and loads of fun, especially the firing of the one o'clock gun, which I found unexpected even though I was expecting it. The gun is fired as a time signal precisely at 13:00 every day, except Sunday, Good Friday and Christmas Day. It was originally established in 1861 as a signal for ships in the harbour of Leith and the Firth of Forth. The castle is a constant procession of museums dedicated to a collection of army battalions, the exhibits interesting and informative. The location of the historic fortress, sat on Castle Rock, dominates the Edinburgh skyline and is now in the care of Historic Scotland. It's the country's most visited paid tourist attraction, with over 1.2 million visitors each year and provides a perfect snapshot of the City's past.

Sarthe, I had been welcomed back, surprising, I know! (October 2014)

I'd been invited back, which was a delightful surprise. On this occasion my immediate reaction was no longer 'Where?' but a more enthusiastic 'Yes, please'. I fell in love with the area on my last visit, especially Le Mans. The whole place resonates an underlying historical aura, so I was more than happy to be back within the Roman Walls of this Plantagenet heartland.

I had returned to look at how the region had progressed with implementing their ambitious plans for the voie vertes (greenways) and their strategic links to the major axis of the European Cycling Plan, both nationally and regionally. I was to expose the 'Sarthe à Vélo' and 'Véloscénie' networks, both in the North West, the Le Mans and La Fleche routes provide access to the Loire à Vélo route. I was also keen to see how the 'Accueil Vélo' accreditation was applied to places to stay. To receive this label certain criteria has to be met:- be within 5km of a cycle route, to have appropriate equipment (secure bike shed, repair kit), to provide a warm welcome with useful information and advice on routes and weather, offer services adapted to cyclists, luggage transfer, washing and drying laundry, bike rental and accessories.

So, after a lengthy trip provided by Brittany Ferries, I and my battered car arrived, slightly jaded, in Le Mans. The plan was to then liaise with Virginie from the Sarthe Developpement, who would transfer me by a better car to the small town of La Fleche for my first overnight stop. After leaving my vehicle in the confines of the underground carpark of the Hotel Charleston I discussed with Virginie the plans for cycling the region, her passion was unmistakable and she explained what I would encounter over the coming days as she drove. The pedalling would begin early the next day.

I awoke to a ghoulish mist as I pulled back the curtains, I had slept well in the comfortable confines of Hotel le Vert Galant (Accueil Vélo accredited) in the heart of La Fleche. The reception at breakfast was comforting; unfortunately the weather was quite the opposite. The deep mist continued to descend and lay like an eerie ivory carpet across the town. After releasing my bike from the excellent storage area, the plan was to discover the 'Sarthe a Vélo' network, which was going to be an issue considering the weather, so I tentatively departed heading towards the old train station and the start of the voie verte – v47 – La Vallée du Loir a Vélo.

As I arrived at the train station, it appeared that the mist had worsened (if that was possible); thankfully, the route was well signed and I set off on my Sarthe adventure. The surface was rideable and I maintained a good speed through rustic surroundings (as far as I could make out). The route was completely empty, the only contact with humanity was when I had to negotiate a roadway but even then the occasional car was my only company. I was mesmerised by the ornate silvery display created by the mist and the frequent spider's webs, a dazzling tapestry of nature at its best.

As the mist lifted briefly I arrived in Le Lude. The town is like the majority of French domains with the addition of one statuesque structure, Le Château. It's believed to be the most northerly Château de la Loire and still inhabited today so I couldn't ignore a visit. Once through the gates, an elegant building presented itself but only just, as the mist continued to distort my view. The gardens are supposedly one of the highlights, a harmonious combination of French design and English style landscape, with a rose garden, topiary, a labyrinth and botanical walk. Yet, as I stood with my back to the foreboding château, I could barely see twenty metres in front. This made for a peaceful atmosphere, with a surprise appearing around every corner despite the odd trip hazard, creating an unexpected meditative setting with a hint of ghostly apparitions. Unfortunately my arrival was before midday and I was too early for a guided tour so after a spritely gloomy wander around the elegant terrace, I departed.

My immediate attention was Vaas, I continued on the v47 (signed La Vallée du Loir a Vélo) south of Le Lude. The route took me on some effulgent country lanes, the views were remarkable as the mist finally disappeared. I halted briefly on the edge of the village, the setting so tranquil with the River Loir dominating the vista, it was undeniably picturesque. After an overdue coffee stop I headed towards Château du Loir now on the v44 (La Sarthe a vélo). The route was once again fixated by vigorous greenery, the gentle noise of slow flowing water and open farmland. I breezed through Château du Loir; the sun was now high in the sky, with no clouds to block its incessant rays. I headed north out of the town to my overnight stop in the village of Beaumont-Pied-de-Boeuf. The D63 was busier than I was expecting but still relatively sedate. Rural France is all about the desolation (in a good way). Quaint hamlets bypassed by rustic roadways, the ubiquitous derelict vehicle, clucking chickens, the weary but adored dog and always a pair of Y-fronts hanging up in the yard – it's a sublime mix of lethargy and more lethargy, and it's infectious.

I arrived in Beaumont-Pied-de-Boeuf around mid-afternoon. My overnight stop at Auberge Relais du Cheval Blanc was hard to miss as it was the only hotel in the village and is a perfect incarnation of a quaint rural domain. After locating my room, I went off to explore. The hotel has an enticing outdoor terrace with a tantalising swimming pool (warm but not that warm). Nearby there is a charming 13th century church with an imposing elevated view of the village. That evening I was immersed in a feast of local produce, delicious scallops and succulent veal, the highlight of a sublime culinary ensemble.

I was up early again; the weather was misty and, after a rapid petit déjeuner, I was off. My goal: the bright lights of Le Mans. First, I would have to negotiate the Forêt de Bercé (Forest). Immediately the terrain became more undulating with gradual inclines and rapid descents. An appointment had been made for me to see the Carnuta in the village of Jupilles. It's a completely new educational concept which has a wealth of exhibits to awaken your senses about man and the forest. Unfortunately I was too early for my appointment and eager to press on so declined and continued on into the magical surroundings of the forest.

The sun was starting to rise amidst the mist which created a mysterious backdrop to the vast expanse of wilderness. The Forêt de Bercé has been recognised for centuries as one of the most absorbing natural areas in France. It's occupied by oak trees, with some being over three hundred years old. As I pedalled I saw countless trails which would happily occupy the explorer types. The temperature was warm and my legs happily churned out the kilometres ably assisted by Radiohead in my headphones, the wooded terrain making the lure of the open road irresistible. I could imagine it holding mysterious, magical powers. Le Grand-Lucé was awash with locals as I entered the main square, the market was in full swing. The animated noise and salivating aromas and perfumes were hypnotic. The car was relegated to a mere bystander as the roadways were preoccupied with the residents haggling over an array of local produce brimming from makeshift boxes. I halted briefly, exchanged salutations with several locals before sitting within the confines of the simple but sacrosanct local church for a moment of contemplation.

Batteries recharged, I headed north east towards Le Mans following the dependable v44. The route again dissected wide open rolling farmland, I briefly skirted the outskirts of luscious woodland before arriving in the busy Parigné-l'Evêque. I freewheeled down to the church and secured my bike. The Church Notre-Dame-de-l'Assomption is a rapturous building originally constructed in the 15th century. The white stone façade so pronounced against the deep blue of the sky, the clarity of the light was magnificent. The town had plenty of agreeable cafés and restaurants, so I stopped for a coffee at the intersection of several busy thoroughfares. For the first time, the roads appeared cluttered with commercial or industrial vehicles chugging laboriously towards Le Mans.

I continued to follow the v44 to my next destination. I again negotiated some mysterious forests and breezed through Changé, the place being deserted; in complete contrast to my last visit when a bustling market was being held in the now empty square. L'Arche de la Nature (translates as Ark of Nature) is 450 hectares of forest and woodland on the edge of Le Mans. I was now sat on the perimeter, replenishing my fluids, looking deep into the heart of the tree cover, the natural lie of the foliage creating an enticing tunnel of discovery, the stillness so apparent. I pushed on, the Plantagenets were now close by. The tarmac was replaced by gravel which only added to the experience, the crunch of the wheels as they collided with the debris evoked childhood memories.

Eventually I emerged from the tree cover by the entrance to the Abbaye l'Épau. I was scheduled to make a visit to the former

Cistercian abbey founded by Queen Berengaria in 1229, but I preferred to spend the afternoon in the heart of Le Mans. I followed the v44 signs towards the train station, weaving through traffic with ease before stumbling on the utterly breathtaking Cathedral. I am the most inappropriate person to be writing this article because no matter how hard I try – I am biased, completely in love with this area. I adore France but this place is like a second home to me. It's as simple and straight forward as that.

I pedalled around the city with memories of my last visit gradually flooding back, the Cité Plantagenêt was as preoccupying as always. Its narrow labyrinthine cobbled streets conquered by lively blossoms and medieval façades. The commercial streets were thronging with locals enjoying the fine weather, drinking and dining al fresco as they intruded onto the pavements. La Place de la République is my favourite location to sit and watch, I happily take on the role of an apprentice voyeur. It evokes a bewitching chaos, a collection of trams, people, bikes and fairground rides sit comfortably amidst the day-to-day monotony of daily life.

I made sure I completely immersed in all things Le Mans before returning to the Hotel Charleston and collecting my car to begin another part of the French adventure. I was en route to Alençon and the Sarthe's neighbour, l'Orne.

Monkey Boy on the South West Coast (June 2014)

If I had a bucket list, top of that list would be to finish my coastal odyssey before I reach the ripe old age of 50 (or ANCIENT, in the simple words of the kids). Annually in July, I resign myself to the extremely unpredictable path of adventure. The physical challenge was never going to be a problem but the desire to accomplish things outside my comfort zone had genuinely surprised me. My previous two outings had opened my eyes to what a delightful island it is that I call home. It made me realise how big the world is and how much we actually see of its beauty, the UK is only a small part of this global family, of which I had been exposed to relatively nothing. I am constantly compelled to learn, discover, impart and this explains perfectly my reasoning for this journey of adventure. I was confident; Devon and Cornwall would provide another individual and original travel experience.

Leaving Dorset and the dazzling Jurassic Coast firmly behind, I hoped Devon would offer similar attractions and enchantments. The county appears to be preoccupied with a bizarre fascination with its close neighbour, across the Tamar. This is perfectly highlighted by the whole 'Cream Tea' debate, in brief, is it cream first or jam first? This simple question causes heated discussion in every household across the South West. Devon is acknowledged as the third largest of the old English Counties behind South Yorkshire and Lincolnshire and my hope was that this portion of the ride would provide me with some pretty beaches, wild scenery, National Parks, rustic villages and towns, historic buildings and well preserved ruins. The county's rich and varied landscapes are rightly treasured by locals and visitors alike and have been recognised with five Areas of Outstanding Natural Beauty, one UNESCO Biosphere Reserve and one UNESCO Geopark, along with two National Parks. Highlights include the dramatic and spellbinding Dartmoor and Exmoor, the steep wooded gorges of the Tamar Valley, West Devon's Mining Heritage, and of course the shapely Jurassic Coast.

I had briefly considered wild camping on Dartmoor. The idea of just pitching up and spending the night under the stars with only wild ponies as company was appealing, particularly the practice of waking to some bohemian views. Dartmoor is one of only a few locations in the country where it is legal to wild camp; as long as you choose your spot sensibly (the sensible bit might be a step too far for me!) Unfortunately my enthusiasm waned significantly following exposure to the harsh weather conditions over the Easter period. Ok, I was completely wimping out and didn't fancy facing elements of the unpredictable British weather. Good quality star gazing requires clear skies, and this could not be relied upon, well that's my excuse!

With Cornwall, my hope was to discover a county of great passions, bizarre customs and romantic Arthurian tales and legends. The attraction is its individuality. The River Tamar cuts off the county completely from the rest of Britain, and this physical barrier has created a place, like no other, with its own language, customs, outlooks and attitudes. Cornwall was predominately created around the prosperous tin and copper industries, nowadays the skyline is subdued by ghosts of its past, a prestigious industrial past.

My travel arrangements had again been dealt with so proficiently by my ageing PA, my father. Unfortunately, my father's debilitating illness had made us change our normal travel plans. The motorhome was no longer a feasible option so Pops had arranged rooms at strategically located Travelodge's along the route.

The plan was to depart from Lyme Regis and end the day on the English Riveria, in Torquay, then onto Plymouth for the second night. The third night we would spend with my auntie and uncle in Falmouth. The last night I was hoping to either wild camp or find a site after circumnavigating Lands End and heading North, eventually meeting up with the support crew somewhere near Redruth, the following day. My route would sporadically reacquaint myself and the bike with the NCN 2 which I had followed all the way from Dover. This long distance cycle route will eventually link Kent with St. Austell in Cornwall. There are still some major gaps in this route, notably between Dawlish and Totnes, and Plymouth and St Austell. Recently, I had discovered the stretch between Exeter and Poole is also signed as part of the Tour de Manche circular cycle route, which links the South West of England with Cherbourg and Roscoff in Northern France. This new concept established in June 2013 consists of two cross-border routes, the Tour de Manche (blue line on the map) and Petit Tour de Manche (red line).

Tour de Manche is a 1200km long itinerary; following the coastline of Brittany through the famous Pink Granite Coast and Cap Fréhel. It links up Brittany and Normandy to Dorset and Devon, and the Petit Tour de Manche, 450km, is an epic journey along the Dorset Jurassic Coast and across the Channel to the Mont St-Michel, both sites classified as world heritage by UNESCO. Offering a visit of the Emerald Coast, the Vire Valley and one of France's Regional Parks, you can stop-over in fascinating Jersey or go on to discover the D-Day

Beaches of Normandy. I feel the need to add this to my ever expanding To-do-List!

If you have read my previous installments on the ride, you would be aware I have made an extremely long 'rod for my own back' by getting the kids to set me challenges for along the way. This year was no exception, after a discussion with Sarah, it was agreed that the kids could each suggest one place I had to visit along the proposed route. Predictably their imaginative minds worked mischievously overtime, resulting in five locations that we eventually agreed upon. Noah wanted me to venture to Torquay Football Club, Eli was adamant I should visit the Minack Theatre, Rosie was the most imaginative, deciding I had to find twelve loos in Looe, Lauren was predictably laidback and happy for me to have a picture at Land's End, and, eventually, Evie (with some guidance by Sarah) settled on a visit to the Monkey Sanctuary near Looe; how apt!

Day One – Lyme Regis to Torquay.

I set off westwards from the outskirts of Lyme. I was glad to be able to finally stretch my legs, I had spent longer than anticipated cramped in a hot car in endless traffic. My original plan was to use the Starcross ferry at Exmouth to cross the River Exe, but the weather was radiant and time was not an issue so I opted to go through Exeter instead following the contours of the Exe. The route took me north of Seaton on the A3052 and I negotiated Colyford with ease. I then encountered Ottery St Mary briefly before finding myself on the precarious A30 (not one of my brightest decisions) eventually locating the less frenetic A379 which transported me over the sedate River Exe. Exeter was thankfully behind me aided by the plethora of cycle routes and I happily continued my journey south towards my original destination, Starcross. I stopped for a rest in the beguiling gardens of

Exminster Church, the building was simple in construction and decoration and provided me with an opportunity to briefly escape the harsh realities of modernity. I then managed to capture some graceful images of the mouth of the river in Starcross, the pier was bustling with ferry goers. Depending on the tides, a typical crossing can take between fifteen to twenty minutes. Next I stumbled on Powderham Castle, the home of the Earl and Countess of Devon with its six hundred years of history. The magical setting beside the Exe Estuary makes it the perfect place to spend a fascinating family day out. The castle is set amongst a colony of deer and exposes the visitor to plenty of history as they wander around and within the castle walls. There are lots to see and do and exploration is a definite must. The sun was now extremely overpowering, so I sat in the shade of a large oak tree and replenished my depleted fluid supplies. I continued on, the signs now informed me I was pedalling on the Exe Estuary Trail. I breezed through Dawlish Warren before finding myself in the gripping confines of Dawlish. I halted in a delicate ornate garden area just off the promenade, eventually resting on the seawall munching a Mr Whippy minus the flake. It was an enjoyable sweet reward for some energetic pedalling.

From Dawlish I began to climb in the direction of Teignmouth. The route was a mix of steep climbs and quick descents. As I approached the town the climb offered a real challenge, the steep incline accompanied by 30°C temperatures was intense, but, once I had reached the town sign, the speedy freewheel into the centre was a much needed diversion. I liked Teignmouth. It's auspicious and buzzy with a pleasant setting where the river Teign meets the sea and is elevated by its proud Victorian pier jutting out into the water. I always find these structures so emblematic of a good old British seaside holiday but it wasn't until the early ninteenthth century that the pleasure pier was born. Nowadays they are a pre-requisite of any seaside town and play a key role in attracting the holidaymakers, with plenty of preservation societies ensuring they are maintained to their original glory. The commercial area had a good array of high street stores interspersed by plenty of independent outlets, a favourable place to browse. The beach was bustling with partially clad tourists, the smell of barbeques wafted in the air. The heat encouraged me into a brief dip. Unsurprisingly, the hill out of Teignmouth was a killer but, at the top, I was treated to a view of Labrador bay which was more than adequate recompense. This RSPB reserve boasts resplendent views, capturing the impressive contours of the coastline over Lyme Bay. I had noticed the familiar acorn sign which pinpoints the South West Coastal Path, the bramble lined trail hugs the top of the cliffs, as it snakes into the distance. After a brief rest I continued on, overhead, unseen birds created a cacophony of noise. A jaunt further on, I reached the outskirts of Torquay.

My immediate focus was Plainmoor, home of the town's football club. Thankfully, the ground was well signposted and, after a short climb, I stood amongst a mass of houses outside the main entrance. After accosting a group of bemused teenagers, a photo was produced as evidence for Noah and I happily pedalled off to locate my bed for the evening. In hindsight I was ripe for a ubiquitous photo-bomb but thankfully the lads behaved. My faith in the youth of today was firmly bolstered.

Torquay is a smart cosmopolitan spot, with modern yachts crowding the harbour. I sat by the water, drinking coffee in one of the many restaurants playing host to smartly dressed diners in animated conversation. When the sun is shining, there is nowhere better than a traditional British seaside resort. It offers a harmonious blend of cutting edge design and naive basic beauty. Ok the weather helped but I did feel so relaxed in the town.

It was early evening as I sat looking across the harbour, the setting sun glistening off the English Riveria Wheel. It was enchanting and, considering the scenic grandeur, the atmosphere was unspoiled and homely. In view of its size, sixty metres tall, the wheel happily blends into the surroundings. It's situated in the Pavillion Gardens and a trip takes approximately twelve minutes. It's notably silent in operation and offers a three hundred and sixty degree bird's-eye view of the town and its coastline. The town forms part of the Torbay triangle which also includes Brixham and Paignton. Torquay is the largest of the three towns and each has its own identity and offers something different to visitors. As I headed back to the hotel I stumbled on a lively brass band entertaining the throng of tourists in the shadows of the wheel. I stopped to enjoy the melodic composition; their repertoire was patterned until my ears were exposed to the abnormal harmony of the Christmas favourite, 'Oh come all ye faithful'. It somehow seemed appropriate but I'm still unsure why.

Day Two – Torquay to Plymouth

Torquay early morning was alluring, a totally different perspective from the previous evenings tourist filled fervour. There were still plenty of people milling around the main harbour area but it was not hard to escape the crowds. I stopped in the beguiling surroundings of Corbyn's Beach with its sparkling bedecked beach huts and just sat transfixed on the water, the odd dog walker as my only company. Paignton is only a short pedal ride along the coast and, considering it was still early, the beach and town were heaving with raucous crowds. My plan was to meet my parents at the steam railway and take the train to Kingwear before arriving in Dartmouth via the ferry. I was a little early so I had time to explore. The town's beach and old harbour appeared to be its major attraction; the shopping area is now dated but offered the usual selection of high street stores and a wealth of cafés and restaurants. The town's name is derived from Paega's town, the original Celtic settlement. I sat with a takeaway coffee in the heart of the bustle at the intersection of several heaving thoroughfares, a throng of tourists completely overwhelmed, created a sublime controlled chaos.

Eventually it was time to be seduced by the Paignton to Dartmouth Steam Railway. The route follows the contours of the triumphant coast down into the Dart Valley and Kingswear which is located at the mouth of the River Dart. The journey covers seven scenic miles and offers some bewitching views, especially of Goodrington Sands as the train squeezes the rugged coastline. Remnants of Brunel are scattered everywhere, the viaducts at Broadsands and Hookhill provide a remarkable visual insight into the Victorian past. It was like stepping back in time, staff adorning traditional costumes, the sound of the steam engine chugging through the enticing landscape. The whole operation is so well run, I was pleased to discover that it is believed to be the most successful heritage railway in the UK, with fully paid staff instead of purely volunteers. This makes it a sustainable tourist attraction, and the commitment and dedication is a credit to all associated with this heritage gem on the Devon coast. I said farewell to my parents, our next interaction would be Wednesday evening in Falmouth, and as I awaited the ferry to take me across the Dart, I was mesmerised by the beauty of Dartmouth, the plethora of quaint houses clinging precariously to the hillside is enthralling. The town is steeped in naval history, it excretes a seafaring legacy. It enthusiastically hugs the quay, its heart is indubitably focused around the enclosed harbour. I walked along the quayside, admiring the vibrantly decorated boats moored up. The town is visually pleasurable with a cluster of old buildings being home to not so old businesses. The historic port is brimming with some handsome boutique style shops, galleries and bistro restaurants, interspersed with a bewitching collection of timber framed buildings, which cascade down to the idyllic water. It was festooned with an array of colourful flowers. The narrow streets are a joy to amble at leisure and there is plenty to explore especially considering the harbour has always been of strategic importance as a deep water port. The road out of the town took me past the Royal Naval College and up a reasonably steep gradient. After the extended rise I eventually began to pick up pace and as I breezed through Stoke Fleming I had a brief interaction with a jovial over-tanned old chap who shouted enthusiastically about the quantity and quality of the local hills. His words were immediately proven as I started a testing climb into dense vivid green trees which offered respite from the glare of the sun. Suddenly and magically I glimpsed an oasis through the branches. A perfect curve of striking blond sand was beckoning to me. It was like a secret world, easily missed enveloped on both sides by luscious tree cover. After an extremely enjoyable descent, I was sat amongst the beach side opulence of Blackpool Sands. The dramatic location, shaded by evergreens and shrubbery has adequate amenities, several cafes and restaurants, toilets and a shop but its greatest appeal is its understated Mediterranean exclusivity, it was a remarkable discovery. Considering the carpark and beach were full with sun worshippers, it still provided a cute homely atmosphere. It is recognised as an award winning privately managed 'Blue Flag' beach. Surveying its beauty, I recognise that the locals probably don't want to encourage too many visitors; it's easy to understand why.

The temptation on a beach like this was just too strong to resist, so with footwear suitably discarded I ventured into watery confines. It was quite nippy but a refreshing relief after the endless climbing in the searing heat. The beach was awash with sun bathers relishing the unusually good weather and who could blame them? It took next to no time for my feet to dry and, after the much needed indulgence, I continued onwards and upwards through the tree cover before descending to sea level, the sudden transition to a level plateau and the beginning of Slapton Ley.

Slapton Ley is an enthralling lake, separated from Start Bay by a shingle beach known as Slapton Sands. It has 1.5 miles of flat roadway and is recognised as a captivating National Nature Reserve and SSSI. The contrast between the tourist traps of Dartmouth and the isolated beaches and coves of Blackpool Sands and Slapton, strikingly devoid of any sign of life, is so beguiling. I headed inland at Torcross on the A379 through Chillington. My progress was delayed by an inviting bakery located in the small hamlet of Frogmore, the shop was the hub of village life. I sat for thirty minutes with a much needed coffee and in that time no fewer than twenty people popped in to grab a coffee, some bread or just for a sociable chat or catch up on the local gossip. It had not gone unnoticed that my journey westwards had now become laboured, due mainly to the incessant heat and the persistent inclines.

From Frogmore the route took me through Kingsbridge, a sleepy market town which offers a valuable insight into rural Devon. It's a marvellous spot to enjoy the extensive multitude of adventure sports on offer, coasteering, body boarding, kayaking etc., the list is endless. I then negotiated Aveton Gifford with ease, before finding myself confronted with a monster climb in Modbury. In fact the climb is the only memorable thing about the town. I stopped for another coffee at a rustic garden centre in the village of Yealmpton. The complex was busy with shoppers wanting the artisan produce on offer, the deli happily dispensed a diverse selection of goods from olives, specialist cheeses and wines to posh quiches and, most importantly, a reasonably priced coffee and some much needed shade.

The achievement I felt when I eventually glimpsed the city sign for Plymouth was profound. A mixture of huge climbs and the sweltering heat had taken their toll. I was exhausted both mentally and physically. Plymouth is a energetic city, I quickly found myself in the heart of its marine heritage, the Barbican. Bubbling with people socialising around the quayside, the perpetual traditional seafaring inns hosting satisfied diners, it was amazing and so captivating. Today the area is home to some exquisite timber framed buildings juxtaposed with some compelling modern attractions and structures. It was only a short mild climb up onto the infamous Hoe.

Plymouth Hoe is famous for its association with Francis Drake and a simple game of bowls, but nowadays it offers an outstanding grassy expanse, home to a proficient collection of ornate memorials and the colourful Smeaton Tower lighthouse. The immediate area was full of people enjoying the good weather. I sat by Drake's Statue, the elevated panoramic views across the Plymouth Sound were absolutely breathtaking, it was easy to imagine Drake and a flotilla of sailing vessels embracing the breakwater.

I left the city, my destination was Saltash and the only obstacle was the River Tamar. I had established the river takes its name, according to legend, from the goddess who was transformed by her father into a river for refusing his suggested suitors. I was astounded by the fact that the Roman Legions never actually crossed the river.

My route took me along the busy A39 dissecting several residential areas. I had to leave Devon and enter Cornwall before I could relax for the evening in Saltash which meant I would have to negotiate the Tamar Road Bridge. The Saltash is one of Cornwall's oldest boroughs, with its waterside inhabited for over a thousand years, and has long been recognised as the 'Gateway to Cornwall'. Saltash is most noted for its two famous bridges: Brunel's Royal Albert Rail wrought iron bridge and the more modern Tamar road bridge. It was an absolute joy to pedal over the road bridge; it provides first-rate views of Brunel's iconic structure and the river below. Its presence is heart stopping. I had read that it was built high above the water to allow tall masted ships to pass beneath. With a collection of narrow streets which rise steeply from the riverbank, the town offers a main street crammed with shops and restaurants. I ate like a king in the local Indian restaurant before a much needed early night.

Day Three – Plymouth to Falmouth

The next morning I was up early, I wanted to see the newly erected Cornish Cross. The cross marks the gateway between Devon and Cornwall and is a deserving addition to the nearby iconic Tamar road and rail bridges. It provides an impressive contemporary welcome to thousands of visitors daily and was opened by Richard Madeley and Judy Finnigan of Richard and Judy fame. The selection did produce a bemused expression from me; my underlying thoughts occupied with the fact there must be somebody better suited or more appropriate.

Just a short walk from the cross is an inconspicuous statue commemorating Isambard Kingdom Brunel, the designer of the nearby rail bridge. Set just off a busy roundabout, it provides a fitting memory to the exploits and visionary skills of the great man. I sat for a while with my back to the inspirational icon, my thoughts focused on the continuous cavalcade of motor vehicles crossing the border between the two passionate neighbours. For some, the reality of having to pay a toll to cross is a costly daily occurrence but a necessity. I climbed away from the town towards St Germans, the route took me through some attractive shaded tree cover, which was a blessing.

St Germans is most notable for its church which was the largest in the county until the construction of Truro cathedral. The village is an attractive combination of historic buildings, almshouses and the magnificent church. The church was founded as an Augustinian priory and the highlight is the dazzling stained glass of the east window created by E Byrne-Jones.

The dense woodland lanes are prevalent, especially around Seaton which is located a short distance along the coast. It's a place that's easy on the eye, supervised by its shingle deserted beach with only a smattering of modern beach houses overlooking the sea. Once a favourite haunt of the enigmatic smuggler, the refined location at the mouth of the River Seaton provides a delicate vantage point to explore the enticing clifftop walkways. I next encountered Looe Hill, huge lungs and legs of steel were required. I felt decidedly good, like I was riding a secret route. There were no vehicles or people; just me, the bike and some unbelievable views of the rugged and lush landscape.

The next thirty minutes were spent in a blur of country lanes, blistering heat and a lack of any appropriate road signs, I had got myself horribly lost, my defunct inner GPS was misbehaving again. My destination was the Monkey Sanctuary, but it was nowhere to be seen and the lack of any brown tourist signs wasn't helping. The more I thought I was pedalling in the right direction, the more I was actually moving further away. Eventually, by chance I stumbled on the attraction tucked away down a dirt track in the middle of the now monotonous greenery! The Monkey Sanctuary is home to a range of different species of monkeys, all rescued from the UK and international pet trade. It's a charitable organisation and home to the eco-friendly Tree Top Café. It is pricey, but if you try to imagine the entrance fee as a donation to help with upkeep and continued sanctuary of these fascinating furry primates, then it seems more acceptable. With a photo taken as evidence for Evie, I departed.

After a short pedal, I entered Looe and felt immediate drawn to the water, finding myself stood on a simple road bridge. The water shifting between deep blue to an iridescent turquoise, boats happily creating ripples on the pretty quay, a medley of pastel coloured houses built precariously into the hillside. It could only be described as a romantic idyll. Fishing is the lifeblood on the town, it's still very much a working port. The daily catch is auctioned on the quayside every morning satisfying the inhabitants enormous appetite for locally caught seafood. In medieval times, there were two distinct towns on opposite sides of the river. Nowadays, both are connected by the bridge. East Looe is recognised as the home to the fishing part, where shoppers and idlers head to the main thoroughfare, which combines some fetching sixteenth and seventeenth architecture. In addition, there are some captivating historical gems and it has the more established beach. In contrast, West Looe is a lot quieter but still has some inviting restaurants and the best vantage point to see Looe Island, which is run as a nature sanctuary by the Cornwall Wildlife Trust. I felt relaxed in the town, even with the claustrophobic amount of tourists. The town opitimises a good old British holiday, families cooling off in the inviting waters, children frolicking, and old fishing boats returning with their catch. Unfortunately I had to succumb to the fact; Cornwall has become a victim of its own popularity. The relentless overcrowding can be an issue; thankfully, it didn't spoil my experience but, for others, like families or the elderly, the enjoyment may be diluted, which is a great shame. I ambled contentedly before visiting the Old Guildhall museum which dates from 1500 and provides an insight into the town's history. Whilst consuming another coffee, I suddenly remembered Rosie's task, finding twelve loos was going to present a problem, mainly because of time. I devised a cunning plan, I would locate a public convenience take a photo as evidence and then go into the first eleven cafes/restaurants along the main thoroughfare and bizarrely ask to take photos of their toilets. As you can imagine my enthusiasm gradually waned after the initial discovery of the stereotypical urine smelling public W.C. so I gave my word to Rosie that the task had been completed, explaining the lack of photographic evidence was down to dodgy batteries in the camera (but we will keep that snippet of information between just you and me).

I reluctantly pedalled out of Looe; my aim was to be in St Austell by lunchtime. I had made a decision to sidestep both Polperro and Fowey, my reasoning was simply one of geographical familiarity. To be fair I had enjoyed my previous visit to both, they offer an abundance of Cornish charm, but equally they also sit at the bottom of very steep energy sapping hills. So, with the heat, plus tired legs, I had chosen to cut across land, initially on the B3359. My destination was Lostwithiel. My only natural barrier was the River Fowey which I easily negotiated by the Lostwithiel train station. The roads in and around the town were blocked with a conveyor belt of motor vehicles. I had read a piece describing Lostwithiel as a small charming town often overlooked by the traveller in a hurry. Unfortunately on this occasion I was guilty of such actions, for which I would like to apologise. I now found myself pedalling on the A390 towards Par. Once I had spotted the signs for the town it was only a short ride into St Austell. The centre was also crammed with vehicles so I took brief respite in the confines of Cemetery Park. I lent the bike against the sundial in the heart of the verdant surroundings. The glistening, modern, sleek and contemporary lines radiating a striking feel good factor, which was a perfect antidote to the suffocating urban environment, a stone's throw through the trees.

Those seeking retail therapy will surely linger at St Austell's eclectic shopping centre, it's full of the usual high street stores but mixed with the reassuring knick knack independents. I ditched my bike by Holy Trinity Church and wandered, stopping briefly for a cheap takeaway coffee. The town had not changed since my last visit, the only difference was that partially clothed locals had replaced the bobble hats and heavy overcoats. I continued on following the B3273 and the contours of the St Austell river, the route enclosed by an extensive wooded enclave until I reached Pentewan.

The village is a quiet place and nowadays the harbour is entirely cut off from the sea, but at its peak it was a thriving port shipping a third of Cornwall's China Clay. Unfortunately, the rise of nearby Charlestown and Par, gradually brought Pentewan's status to an abrupt decline and in the 1960's the last boats entered the harbour. Today the village is regulated by the modern phenomenon of the Pentewan Sands Caravan and Camping site. The site and the beach are nestled in the pleasant setting of Mevagissey Bay and provides relatively safe conditions for swimmers and water sports enthusiasts. From Pentewan I started a gradual climb towards Mevagissey, the views of the bay below were spectacular. The descent into the traditional Cornish village was a mix of exhilaration tinged with a little speedy apprehension.

The crowds can overwhelm, especially at weekends and during the summer months, and today was no exception. The sun shaded narrow back streets were bustling with partially clad tourists, buffeted by a cooling wind. It created a supreme portal into the past, with nets made of natural materials and sanguine buoys hung over tiny intricate doorways. The harbour was scorched by the sun, the majority fighting for the sparse shade. My previous encounter of Mevagissey was on a dark early December morning. On that occasion, I had written about the serene tranquility, a relaxing hideaway, and that my reaction would probably be completely different when presented with an influx of rowdy tourists and polluting motor vehicles. To be honest, the mass of bodies didn't ruin the experience but, selfishly, I missed having the charming harbour to myself. I only lingered long enough to consume a quick coffee and, as the temperature continued to rise, I pushed on along the coast. Unfortunately, my first task was to negotiate the substantial climb out of the village, heading south towards Gorran Haven. This section of the coastline is punctuated with an eye-opening collection of craggy coves and rocky outcrops. I headed briefly inland and hurried through Gorran Churchdown, when suddenly a secluded bay unravelled before me.

The shimmering water of Porthluney Cove and the forlorn castle of Caerhays were both attractive and married well. The area was bereft of any human life. This stretch of coastline offers a wealth of enticing bays and coves to explore, some well-known but others invisible to only a select few locals, brilliantly opitimised by the words of Shakespeare 'England bound in with the triumphant sea whose rocky shore beats back the envious siege of watery Neptune'.

I could just glimpse the castle in the distance, as I stood by the roadway. I had read that the highlight is the spring gardens set in one hundred and twenty acres of woodland. Unfortunately a sign stated it was closed but thankfully I had the sublime views of the cove as recompense. I was now firmly entrenched in the Roseland Peninsula, which affords a provocatively aesthetic pastoral landscape surrounded by water on three sides. A maze of deserted country lanes winding through lush woodland and bucolic hamlets, a place to travel slowly and savour the magical views of the Fal Estuary.

St Mawes was my gateway to Falmouth. The quaint fishing village sits in the shelter of its castle and is a lesser known but pretty part of the Roseland Peninsula, only separated from Falmouth by a mass of water. It's discernibly one of Cornwall's best kept secrets with a postcard perfect secluded harbour which still looks to the sea for its livelihood.

There's no better way to arrive in Falmouth than aboard a boat. I spent a gleeful twenty minutes on the St Mawes Ferry, bobbing across the Carrick Roads, sea spray soothing my sun soaked arms. The area is rich in folklore, superstitions and traditions and my mind was preoccupied by the legend of Morgawr, a sea monster which is supposed to live in Falmouth Bay and, according to the myth, the beast prefers hot summers and calm waters, so the conditions were conducive for an impromptu appearance. We passed the enigmatic castle of St Mawes, one of King Henry VIII's coastal fortresses which sits imposingly overlooking the waters. As we approached Falmouth I was surprised by the size of docks. It's recognised as the third largest natural deep water harbour in the world and today only reinforced its credentials, with the sight of a large cruise liner in temporary residence. I was especially impressed by the neat architecture of the multi award winning National Maritime Museum which provides a modern striking backdrop to the busy harbour. The port has played a major seafaring role since Tudor times when Henry VIII built two castles to protect the entrance to its harbour. Nowadays the town is still a thriving port with water activity all year round. It happily plays host to plenty of cafés, restaurants, galleries and shops, and is even home to the emblematic Cornish flagship retail experience, Trago (or Trago Mills).

My base for the night was my aunt and uncle's house in a quiet suburban housing estate near the Penmere area of the town. That evening, my aunty cooked the best grilled fish I had ever tasted, locally caught fish which we consumed by the sea. How lucky was I. The single minded Cornish outlook of 'Cornish is best' is so laudable and a credit to its citizens. Logically, why not use local produce? It creates revenue and promotes laudable community spirit which can be found nowhere else, in my opinion. Big thumbs up to the Cornish ideology! Another of my aunts many talents is her brilliance at providing directions, the human equivalent of Google Maps. I acknowledged her skills as I dropped into a deep overdue sleep.

Day Four – Falmouth to Lands End

With my aunt's directions firmly planted in my grey matter I set off for Land's End, first I had to negotiate Asda (thanks aunty) then Helston and Penzance. I followed the busy A394 all the way into Helston. The town was larger than I had anticipated with a busy main shopping street full of the usual delights. To be honest the town didn't inspire, regrettably the past three days had exposed me to the charm soaked attractions of south Devon and Cornwall and this made Helston seem sadly lacking, which is a shame. After stopping for some sustenance, I pushed on towards Penzance continuing on the A394.

The riding was comfortable with the occasional climb but mostly prostrate roadways. The sun was intense and high in the sky as I approached Penzance. I left my bike secured by the harbour and went off to explore, my reward a well-earned breather. The town is a mix of Georgian and Regency townhouses, with an abundance of high street stores, although the fine architecture is undermined by the slightly faded shopfronts. The highlight is the Humphry Davy statue and the ornate Market House situated on Market Jew Street. Humphry Davy is the town's most famous son and was responsible for an astonishing amount of pioneering scientific advances. He also contributed to the local mining industry and is known as the inventor of the Miners Safety Lamp or Davy Lamp. The town is located at the northern end of Mounts Bay, I sat with a coffee on the harbour front, the view of the eye catching St Michaels Mount was magical. Built as a Benedictine Priory in 1135 and dedicated to the Archangel St Michael, it marks the mystical southern end to the pilgrims route, St Michaels Way.

From Penzance the landscape changed dramatically, I was now presented with an array of treeless fields separated by simple ornate drystone walls. Remnants of early man inconspicuously dotted the landscape, mystical stone circles and ancient religious sites providing an interesting vision into how the landscape and the elements shaped the area and affected the inhabitants.

Land's End is synonymous with the increasing popular ethos of charity bike rides. The feeling for me was one of deflation. The site is now home to a collection of tourist attractions and fast food restaurants. It was nice to see the iconic Land's End signpost (which provided me with the evidence of my visit for Lauren) and the unsurpassed views of the granite cliffs and the sea were remarkable, but unfortunately its infamy is its major failing. The car park was congested, the crowds overbearing, the romantic notion of the last piece of England somewhat spoiled. Although there was one attraction that I would recommend, The End to End Story. The free exhibition is crammed with facts on the feats intrepid adventurers put themselves through to complete the LeJog (Land's End to John O'Groats) challenge.

I sat and daydreamed, the air rich with the smell of seaweed and salt. I wandered in and out of the gift shops and eventually left as the crowds became an annoyance. As I exited the car park, I noticed the signs for the Cornish Way, the start/finish point of the NCN 3. My next destination was in fact two places but with a magical connection, a short pedal along the coast is the magnificent Porthcurno Beach which is overlooked by the equally magnificent Minack Theatre.

I always thought a beach is just a beach, a collection of sand, tepid water and a congregation of sun worshippers in stages of redness but with Porthcurno my opinions changed dramatically. I was exposed to the most luminescent blue waters and clean, nearly blonde, sand I thought only possible in movies. There were plenty of bronzed bodies on the beach and the whole atmosphere was bubbling with an infectious Mediterranean influence. I sat with footwear removed and just lazed, which is an alien concept to me. With my preconceptions firmly shattered I pushed off the short distance up an extremely steep incline towards the theatre of dreams.

The Minack Theatre offers unobstructed views of the terrific Porthcurno Beach, arguably the most seductive beach in the country, if not the world. The open air theatre is perched on the sheer cliffs and is a triumph of the vision of its creator, Rowena Cade. It offers a unique appreciation, just the opportunity to sit and watch the sea with some magnificent vertiginous views was staggering. Most importantly, it also gave me the chance to successfully complete my final task, so as I happily snapped away I hoped Eli would be pleased. My only regret is that I didn't have the opportunity to see a performance. The summer theatre season runs from May to September presenting an eclectic mix of drama, musicals and opera. I had read that Minack means 'Rocky Place' in Cornish which is so apt considering its many crags. From 1931 until her death in 1983 the theatre was planned, built and financed by Rowena, her passion and commitment is admirable and appears to gush from its foundations. It's a sensational setting to just amble around the collection of well-presented gardens and a pit stop is highly recommended at the café with similarly confounding vistas of the coastline rising majestically from the water. The only downside is its unique attraction, the location could provide access problems for the elderly or infirm but otherwise a visit is a must, especially after the disappointment of Land's End.

Technically I had come as far as I wanted on this part of the Monkey Boy ride. I retraced my way back to Falmouth. I had decided an uncomplicated sleep at my relatives was more attractive than an uncomfortable sweaty night under canvas. The decision was a resounding success as my aunty introduced my mum and I to the allurement of Swanpool beach.

Swanpool is the ultimate alfresco location, set amidst the hustle and bustle of suburbia. A great spot to relax and people watch! It oozes a seductive spirituality. A place that has been, thankfully, forgotten by time, only briefly and delicately touched by the minimal of modern intrusions. I was smitten, the laidback lifestyle was so addictive. As the sun set, the last of its rays created a phenomenal red glow on the nearby rocks. This place can evidently inspire. I wonder if they would allow me to build my own beach shack, accessorised with sleepy hammock, barbeque and an over-used turbo trainer? A simple retreat, with the beauty of the sea as a most attentive neighbour. I would like to thank my aunty for introducing me to the fascinations of this unspoiled location!

The past four days had introduced and immersed me in everything that is great about our small diverse nation. Where else can you experience so much without having to travel great distances, like in other parts of the world. In my opinion when the weather is behaving, there is nowhere better than the home grown appeals of Britain. I would like to thank my aunty and uncle for their hospitality, they made us most welcome and provided us with the opportunity to relax as a family and enjoy each other's company, unhindered and stress free for the very last time before my father's passing. Devon and Cornwall will hold so many memories for me, unsurprisingly all good. The magical beaches, the incomprehensible locals, the myths and legends, the hypnotic cinematic landscapes, the quaint picture postcard villages and hamlets and on this occasion the sublime weather. It was a joy!

On my next outing, I will be focussing on the West coast of Cornwall and Devon and maybe even touching on Somerset. Unfortunately the sensation will be minus one incredible character, my father, his death has made me a much stronger individual and so determined to see this epic journey through to completion. My goal, with which Bazza would have agreed, is to enjoy every minute. Life is a journey, it's about experiences – sometimes good and sometimes bad – and we should embrace everything that is thrown in our path because, ultimately, that's what makes us who we are and how we live.

I simply love Connemara (January 2015)

New Year's Day is always an anti-climax, all the partying of the festive period (which invariably lasts at least a week) is over and even the normally frenetic dog is overwhelmed with a lethargic malaise. As I sat watching some naff movie, I pondered my first trip of the year. My invite to the West side of Ireland was two-fold; to understand the Wild Atlantic Way and pedal along a section of the Tour of Connemara. My knowledge was limited (it was in fact non-existent) so I did what most would do and scanned the ubiquitous internet. What I found was more than promising with glowing reviews, alluring images and bewitching descriptions of wild untouched coastlines, epitomised by the following passage. "Where land and sea collide, where untamed beauty abounds, welcome to the unforgettable experience of the Wild Atlantic Way" I was sold, who wouldn't be after those evocative words?

Our transportation was provided by Aer Lingus, the flight from Heathrow to Shannon was short, fuss-free and comfortable and we arrived at midday. The weather was cold, but the sun had decided to provide a preposing bright Irish hello.

The Wild Atlantic Way is a tourism trail on the west coast of Ireland. The 2,500 km (1553 miles) driving route passes through nine counties and three provinces, stretching from County

Donegal's Inishowen Peninsula to Kinsale, County Cork, on the Celtic Sea coast. Along the route there are places and attractions which have been designated as points of interest for travellers. Our destination was Connemara, a wild and barren district in the west, just north-west of Galway.

The plan was loose, but would involve some interactions with two wheels, I was accompanied by my wife whose role was to capture a mix of bikes and the unspoilt rugged surroundings, simple! Unfortunately, we were travelling in the middle of January, so the weather would provide some distinct problems, with the possibility of being exposed to some extremely harsh conditions a definite reality. As well as interacting with the Wild Atlantic Way, we were here to also savour the route (or part of the route) of the Tour of Connemara before the 2015 event on 23 May.

Our destination was Clifden, and after a two hour drive through Galway and dissecting some awesome panoramic views we arrived mid-afternoon. The town is the largest in Connemara with a population of twelve to thirteen but, in the summer months, this increases ten-fold. There are plenty of pubs and traditional shops, Clifden is a small charming town renowned for its traditional nightlife, it's a party town and unofficially classed as the Capital of Connemara.

Our base was the unusual Clifden Station House Hotel which is a cordial place, the location is prime and the staff possess a fantastic mix of typical Irish hospitality and staggering professionalism. The railway line from Galway to Clifden was opened on 1 July, 1895 and there were some thirty bridges, including an imposing steel viaduct. Today the station building and platform have been thoughtfully restored to their original glory and are home to the enchanting hotel. There is a project to develop the old railway line into a cycling and walking trail between Clifden and Galway. The Greenway has two recognised phases; one is to focus on the route between Oughterard and Clifden and two will concentrate on Galway to Oughterard. When complete, it will provide a seventy-eight kilometre traffic free cycle route through this arresting landscape. It proved the ideal base to explore.

The Tour de Connemara starts and finishes outside the hotel; the finish is all taped off and there is an elaborate finishing line where participants receive their medal on a makeshift podium. I had an early morning appointment with one of the organisers of this popular event, Mark O'Connell. Over coffee, we discussed the Tour of Connemara and the general cycling scene in this part of West Ireland. His passion was immediately evident and his company W2 have for several years efficiently organised the sportive. They provide strategic research, planning, evaluation and project implementation specialising in the tourism and sports sectors.

As Mark explained, the event attracts cyclists from all over the world, as well as Ireland. He was chuffed with the amount of riders already registered for the 2015 sportive. Riders can choose to ride either 80km or 140km with majority of participants opting for the 140km with the 80km popular with women. The entry fee is €40 if you are a member of Cycling Ireland and €45 if you are not. This registration gets you a 2015 Skoda Tour de Conamara Gilet, Powerbar products, access to feed stations, bike and medical back up supports, 2015 finishers medal and entry into five draws for great cycling prizes.

It was time to be introduced to my bike, Mark had brought along a Greg Le Mond classic road bike. He enthusiastically explained the heritage but I sort of wish he hadn't. Basically it was Greg Le Mond's very own bike which was given to Mark a few years earlier, what a treat but also a HUGE responsibility. Why was Mark not worried about his pride and joy, especially after my detailed description of the accident on my previous trip to the Midi-Pyrenees? His confidence was reassuring, but hopefully not misplaced, as we negotiated the hotel car park. Mark later told me over lunch that he was following me close by just in case I did fall, when he planned to throw himself in-front of the bike and not me, and rightly so, it's Greg Le Mond's bike after-all. (I do hope he was having the craic).

Thankfully, the weather had reached a reassuring calm as we headed out of town, south over the sea inlet, following the evocative R341 (also signed 'The Wild Atlantic Way'). Over our left shoulders was a cinematic view of Salt Lake. Serenity immediately descended as we left the hustle and bustle of Clifden behind. The road surface was excellent and, as we approached Derrygimia, I remembered that the site of the Marconi Station was close by, as well as the location of the first transatlantic flight made by Alcock and Brown who crash landed unceremoniously in a nearby bog.

Next we encountered Ballyconneely which offers riveting panoramas across the bay with its maze of mesmerizing islands. The whole area is an intricate patchwork of bogs and an unparallelled collection of small lakes that resembled sheet glass as the effects of the sun shimmered off their surface. This section is renowned for its magnificent white beaches and plenty of space to enjoy the waters. We breezed through Errisbeg which has the only significant climb along this stretch of coastline before entering Roundstone. This small fishing village was deserted apart from the odd ageing cyclist; it basically consists of a single main street of tall houses, shops and several pubs. As we pushed on the rain started and the wind become more of a hindrance, but not an annoyance.

The previous night I had spoken in detail with the manager of the accommodation, Ronan, a native of Cork but his passion for Connemara was astonishing. I could listen to him all day, animatedly enthusing about the area and all the key historic sights and great locations to explore. His plans for the hotel were encouraging, especially for us explorer types. His focus is on cycling, adventure racing, trekking and walking, but basically anything that gets you out and gets the air into your lungs. All his plans are viable and will enhance the business internationally and I wish him all the success in the world, he definitely deserves it. Out of season, the hotel offers some attractive deals to keep things ticking over but the summer months are extremely busy, with August always full to capacity. Later in the evening, as we relaxed in the bar, Ronan went off to get me a map and returned with a sufficiently large cumbersome framed map of Connemara. It was slightly comedic as he struggled through the door with arms at full stretch, coining it an 'Irish GPS'. Not sure how I was going to fit it on the bike I told him as we both giggled like naughty children, but I gave him my word I would try!

The lunar landscape was deserted apart from grazing sheep and the odd motor vehicle. The coastline was literally in touching distance, the evocative aromas of fresh seaweed, mixed with a fresh crisp air, invigorated my senses. Interaction through simple smell was a highlight, and stimulated my affection and adoration for this consuming technology-free oasis. A place of utter tranquillity. I was amazed by the space everywhere, absorbed by a simple expanse of greenery tentatively holding off the ferocious and unpredictable power of the Atlantic. The volatile interaction of the two was completely mesmerising and makes the cavalcade of dramatic vistas as alluring and as remarkable as any views I have encountered throughout the world.

The route contoured the coastline on extremely well surfaced roads, the majority tarmaced and strangely no potholes. We were exposed to a magnificent journey of discovery, the isolation was captivating, devoured by open spaces and the odd wild enchanting building hiding a secret simple indulgence. I was hoping to hear the locals speaking in the native tongue (Ireland's Gaeltacht – Irish speaking regions) but our only real interaction was the mass of free roaming sheep. It was close to perfect.

I had read a passage on the Wild Atlantic way which completely optimised the admiration 'Wherever you go along the Wild Atlantic Way, you will encounter moments of magic, moments to treasure and experiences that you will want to return to again and again' – I rest my case!

As we neared the Inagh Valley, the horizon was lavished by ominous cloud cover and unfortunately we had to accept the weather was going to cut our ride short. We paused briefly to survey the views, the outline of 'The Twelve Pins' and the 'Maumturk Mountains' framed the landscape so dramatically. We begrudgingly detoured onto another well surfaced road and pedalled back towards Clifden, hoping the weather would hold off until we returned to a semblance of civilisation. This stretch of roadway is locally referred to as the Greenway and, as I mentioned earlier, work is underway to convert it into a well maintained route, accommodating cyclists and walkers.

Thankfully the flat landscape enabled us to make good speed in our quest westwards. The surroundings reminiscent of an engrossing Snowdonia and Exmoor concoction, rugged and barren with the odd sheep or cow grazing happily, it was a place of total unequivocal solitude. We easily negotiated Arkeen Beg and Arkeen More before reaching the outskirts of Clifden and tedious unwanted reality. I longed for the mystery and peacefulness that I had been exposed to over the previous few hours.

We couldn't leave without experiencing the Sky Road and the Inagh Valley, so, the next morning, as the sun was shining, we followed the signage towards the viewing point on the Sky Road. The encounter was overwhelming, the views from this natural hillside balcony over the Atlantic and the mass of rocky desolate islands and secluded bays has to be one of the most scenic in Ireland. It was a similar realisation as we travelled slowly along the Inagh Valley, the Twelve Pins glowing in the bright sunlight. We couldn't prevent ourselves from stopping like annoying tourists to capture the unbelievable array of photo opportunities. We followed the route through to Kylemore Abbey. The building was built for a wealthy English businessman in the 19th Century, nowadays it is run by nuns as an exclusive convent boarding school with some sections open to the public. It was unfortunately time to leave this graceful place, so, emotionally, we pointed our vehicle in the direction of Galway and Shannon Airport, and our plane home. But we will be back, Connemara has left an imprint on both mine and Sarah's hearts and will always be somewhere we remember fondly.

Unfortunately, I was unable to attend the event on 23 May but I had agreed with Mark O'Connell that Cycling World Ireland would sponsor a competition for a blogger to write a small piece detailing their participation of the ride. That individual, as well as having their words published in a subsequent issue, would also receive a year's subscription to Cycling World Ireland. Who knows, we might uncover a real talent!

Prudential RideLondon, a fun packed family weekend in the capital.
(August 2014)

The Mayor of London's cycling extravaganza was to take place on the weekend of 9 and 10 August, conveniently when I was down in the capital. It's billed as the World's greatest festival of cycling developed by the Mayor of London and his agencies in partnership with Surrey County Council.

It was first held in 2013 and is a combination of top professional road races, amateur cyclists participating in a one hundred mile challenge and a free family ride in the heart of the city. I had been in touch with company dealing with the event and was given access to the Media Centre. The itinerary was exhaustive, with the Cycling show starting on the Thursday and the last ride finishing on the Sunday evening. The event comprised five events, the FreeCycle and Grand Prix on the Saturday. The Sunday was allocated to HandCycle Classic, London-Surrey 100 and London-Surrey Classic.

I arrived on a sun drenched Mall early Saturday morning. The surroundings were already heaving with cyclists of all shapes, sizes, ages and genders. The animated noise and hilarity was so reassuring. As I wandered through Green Park, the numbers increased, with plenty already enthusiastically utilising the services of the plethora of healthy food outlets. The Green Park festival zone was a mass of brightly coloured deckchairs set strategically towards a stage which would host a cavalcade of music performances. It was also home to the Guinness World Records Street Trails Battle, where the World's best stunt riders would battle it out to break records throughout the day; this included the inspirational Andrei Burton. I was enjoying the sense of escape from the bright lights of the city.

Unfortunately I had missed the start of the FreeCycle ride but, with media access, I could get up close when the early riders returned back towards Buckingham Palace or began through Admiralty Arch, lending its distinctive imprint to the skyline. It was great to see families enjoying the pleasant weather whilst pedalling on the empty streets of the capital. The route was ten miles long and passed some of the capitals iconic buildings, Admiralty Arch, Nelson's Column, Tower of London and St Paul's Cathderal. The ethos was great, everybody welcome regardless of age or ability. I especially enjoyed the laidback approach of joining the route at any point and doing as many laps as you wanted, stopping en-route for a pint or to immerse in a range of bike-related entertainment.

As the cyclists increased a bottle neck naturally occurred at Admiralty Arch, they were expecting more than fifty thousand riders throughout the day. This was managed perfectly by the mass of brightly clad marshals. The crowds around Trafalgar Square were astonishing, twenty deep all showing their appreciation and admiration through a constant stream of applause and whoops. I followed the throngs down onto the Embankment, the enjoyment evident on everybody's faces. The view of the London Eye and the Thames as a backdrop was sublime as a conveyor belt of brightly coloured Lycra nonchalantly pedalled by.

As I sat just outside the Embankment tube station in the shadows of Hungerford Bridge, I observed person after person unlock a Barclays Cycle Hire bike and join the party, the urge to cherish the joy and family atmosphere was too overwhelming. It was great to witness this unique camaraderie and acceptance, a joyous coming together of all with no pre-conceptions, something I find rare when I usually visit the capital. As I made my way back up towards Green Park, I was amazed by the amount of BCH bikes being used. The event hopes to demonstrate to the population that cycling can be fun, healthy and have a positive effect on the environment. I have no doubt this event and the legacy of the 2012 Olympics and the Tour will encourage more to venture out on a bike.

Back in the verdant confines of Green Park, I sat and watched the magic of Andrei Burton and a team of madcap stunt cyclists as they attempted some hair-raising tricks in a breath-taking display of skill, dexterity and complete insanity. I eventually had to move to find some shade as the heat soared, the smell of suncream was absolutely everywhere. I then proceeded to mingle with the riders as they approached Buckingham Palace from the Mall. The masses stood with phone in hand to take that memorable selfie as a simple souvenir of their day. The whole atmosphere was one of absolute happiness and collective warmth.

After a short break, inspecting my eyelids under the comfortable tree cover, I was ready to be introduced to the joys of Women's Elite Road Racing. The Grand Prix event was billed as the greatest Womens's criterium ever to be staged in the UK. In the inaugural event staged in 2013, Laura Trott beat Hannah Barnes in a dramatic finish. This year was to end in similar fashion with Giorgia Bronzini of Team Wiggle Honda pipping the reigning World and Olympic champion Marianne Vos on the line, with Lizzie Armitstead a close third. As I watched from a great vantage point on the Mall, I was in awe of the athletic prowess of these dedicated individuals. The pace and commitment was startling, the tension super-charged as the lead changed constantly. The race finished in a furore, as the crowds exploded into crescendo of applause and the riders into the solace of the finish line.

The next day I headed back down to the Mall to see the first riders return after completing the London-Surrey 100. 80,000 cyclists entered the ballot to take part and around 24,000 were envisioned to start the race at the Queen Elizabeth Olympic Park in Stratford. The ride took place on a collection of closed roads in the capital and the picturesque Surrey countryside. Unfortunately due to the awful weather conditions (wet and windy) the two biggest ascents on the route, Leith Hill and Box Hill were dropped, reducing the distance to a soggy eighty-six miles. The dedication of all involved was commendable. Especially impressive was the hardcore spectators, who stood for hours in the incessant rain, cheering everyone with vigour and a heroic resilience.

As the weather worn riders returned, their positive demeanours belied the fact they had been exposed to near torrential, flash flooding rain. They all appeared enthused by their immersion, the British resolve overwhelmingly evident, with the approach 'Oh well, I am wet and I can't get any more wet, so I might as well enjoy it!'.

I was disappointed that I had missed the Handcycle Classic event which began in Kingston-upon-Thames. The fifteen mile race was contested by thirty of the world's greatest handcyclists and was eventually won by Austria's Walter Ablinger. The bad weather had dented my resolve significantly, so I decided, mid-morning, that I would depart the capital after an absolutely memorable few days. This meant I would miss the drama of the top pro Men cyclists battling it out over 200km through the beauty and splendour of the Surrey Hills. In the usual media frenzy, it was announced that both Mark Cavendish and Sir Bradley Wiggins would be competing, in reality, Cavendish had to pull out due to injury and Wiggins finished some way back in the race which was won in a dramatic sprint finish by the mud splattered Adam Blythe pipping Ben Swift on the line.

I was lucky enough to chat to one of the competitors Peter Waterfield, the British diver and Olympic Silver medallist. Peter was riding as Captain for the Mayor's Fund and is no stranger to the start point, the Queen Elizabeth Olympic Park in Stratford.

What was the main reason for agreeing to participate in this year's Prudential RideLondon event?

The Mayors Fund for London asked if I would like to captain their team. When I looked into what they do for young people I had to do it, as they help many young people in lots of different programmes from giving unfortunate kids a healthy breakfast before school (if they don't get it at home), to helping young people find pathways to jobs.

Are you a regular cyclist?

No! Prudential ride London was my first ever ride event and I managed to do four hard thirty-mile training sessions due to some little niggles (injuries), and I completed it in 5 hours 17 min.

Did you enjoy the ride?

Yes I did enjoy it; all my training rides were in the sun, so doing it in the bad weather was tough, but I still really enjoyed it.

What was the best and worst part of the pedalling?

The worst part of pedalling is that I've only ever trained my legs to react and explode fast to jump high with no endurance, so doing a sport like this with minimal training isn't ideal for me but as an athlete my competitive nature got me through the last 10-15 miles.

The best part is how far you can push yourself as there were a couple of times I wanted to walk for a bit, especially up one of the hills.

Who was the most competitive amongst the celebrities?

It certainly wasn't me who was the most competitive, I was in my own competition as I wanted to beat my expectation of myself, as it was my first one I didn't want to get too confident or competitive with everyone.

I was down on the Mall both days and the support was overwhelming. Did this spur you on?

Finishing on the Mall was amazing; the support was great and I had to get to the end because my family was waiting for me, and when I saw them, it made me feel very special.

Were you disappointed the two infamous climbs were dropped from the route?

I was a little disappointed when I heard the two big hills had been taken out, but then, when I struggled with the other steep hill on the ride, I thought, I'm glad they took them out.

Will you be back next year?

Yes, I would love to do it again, but next time I'll be better prepared for it.

Anjou Vélo Vintage, an extravaganza of vintage in the Loire Valley (June 2014)

Feasibly I could simply cheat and cut and paste the press release for this intriguing event, which is well written, informative, visually attractive and enticing. On the other hand, nothing beats the chance to immerse in the sights, smells, interactions, weather and gastronomy of a place, or event, so being there in person felt like a great decision. I would have to describe myself as a fortunate chap, (some might say jammy) there are some pros to being an editor. The chance to explore, and comprehend things others can only dream about, is certainly one of them.

With this great power comes a responsibility to provide a level opinion, without ambiguity and document my experiences good, bad or indifferent. Actually that's all nonsense, it's all about having unadulterated fun which a bike offers in abundance. I was here in the Loire Valley to immerse in all things vintage, and I couldn't wait.

It was my first experience of London City Airport and, on an exceptionally bright warm early morning, we were met by a jovial BA representative. Our destination was Angers Loire Airport, the schedule was created three years ago, and only flies throughout the summer months. Our group consisted of journalists, writers and a photographer, some well-known, and others, like me, blissfully inconspicuous to the relatively small group of other flyers. The flight was brief (only one hour) and we arrived to the rain and gloom of the Loire. I have to admit the grey gloominess of the Loire is a more attractive alternative to its bland and somewhat depressing Anglo cousin.

I will set the scene; L'Anjou Vélo Vintage is a two day retro bike festival for devotees of yesteryear bikes and music. The annual weekend event is set up in the heart of the historic Saumur, which is wedged tightly against the Loire. The Sunday is dedicated to the criterium, four circuits were on offer, 30km, 55km, 90km and a lengthy 150km. What I was to discover would bring me closer to Plantagenet Kings; the Anjou area was the cradle of a powerful medieval dynasty, with its landscapes supervised by a plethora of imposing fortifications. It's also home to some hidden gems, with astonishing caves and quarries peppering the countryside around Saumur. The itinerary was in place, at a glance it could be described as hectic, with a hint of chaos, but hey, life is about experiences and we were not to be disappointed! A feast of cycling, gastronomy and architecture awaited us.

Our first destination was the Cointreau distillery on the outskirts of Angers. It's the only production site of the drink in the world. Its appearance is individually modern and contemporary. The factory is preoccupied by the invigorating aroma of oranges and the décor is overpoweringly orange, for self-explanatory reasons. There was a fun and interesting museum but I was disturbingly preoccupied by the Cointreau family busts, all of whom possessed an alarmingly likeness to Lenin, especially Louisa, the wife of Eduord, one-time owner of the brand.

As we travelled to lunch we were introduced to the Loire à Vélo cycle network which makes its way through the lunar landscape of the outskirts of Angers, coerced by the remnants of the slate industry. As we followed the contours of the Loire, our guide explained enthusiastically that a new trail, which hugs the river, is due to open shortly. Currently the route is someway from the river through farmland, the new route will be a great improvement providing a fascinating immersion in the entrancing waterway. Our host explained that an original way to explore these cycle routes has been devised and called Cyclopedia. It's an application for your smartphone which allows individuals to explore the allures on the Loire à Vélo trail between Gennes and Montjean-sur-Loire by providing a multi media guide coupled with GPS and designed for touring cyclists. The main function is to identify all the highlights along the route which are automatically displayed. The app is available through all App Stores and Google Play. As we continued, we were exposed to some exciting far reaching views of the countryside and its close relationship with the Loire. Less special was the weather, the rain was now relentless.

Lunch was provided by the La Route du Sol restaurant, the unspoilt location on the banks of the Loire did not disappoint, even with the less favourable weather. The menu was delectable, traditionally cooked food but with an international twist, the crayfish was delicious. The afternoon commenced with a sedate boat trip, the captain explaining that the Loire is the longest river in France and admitting that the majority of British tourists visit predominately to the see the birds. Some things don't change. Unfortunately the experience was affected by the now incessant rain so we returned to land, earlier than forseen.

After a brief halt to check in at our hotel in Saumur, we were en route to L'Anjou Vélo Vintage village to choose our bikes for the next day's ride. The rain was offering an unfortunate torrent of watery misery, the mass of bric-a-brac and vintage bikes stalls most noticeably affected by the grey skies. The array of vintage retro bikes was remarkable, standing proudly in the now constant rain, adding to their already rusty appearance. The two keen cyclists in our group, myself and Tim, couldn't contain our excitement, we were like the proverbial 'kids in a candy store'. The rain was no longer an issue, we were oblivious to its deterioration, our concentration elsewhere.

The selection process was surprisingly much harder than you would imagine, with rust, without rust, a mass of rust, drop bar handles, upright handles, leather seat, plastic seat, no seat. I had been informed that the bike frame had two non-negotiable requirements, it had to be pre-1987 and feature no handle bar mounted gear shifters or automatic foot bar. Finally I made a hurried selection, a red skinny racer with minimal brakes and possibly the most uncomfortable plastic seat imaginable. That evening we were exposed to a prodigious Anjou festival, an ensemble of food, swing music, entertainers and acrobats. An all round retro extravaganza within the unique confines of the Bourvet Ladubay caves.

The next morning after a comfortable night's sleep we were delivered to our temporary home, Press Corner. The mass of people and bikes were extraordinary; the weather was behaving, bright blue skies and the sun happily in situ, yesterday's downpour a distant memory. I was astonished by the array of retro costumes; a blanket of colour regulated the horizon as we waited patiently for the pedalling to begin. Unfortunately, it was a stuttered, sluggish departure; still, spirits were high, with smiles and laughter ever present amongst the retro clad congregation. Everyone is encouraged to dress up in a colourful retro style, my commitment was pathetic, a simple Cinelli cycling cap my dismal offering. We gained a gradual momentum as we crossed the start line, perfectly situated alongside the peaceful Loire. I had opted for the 55km route and as we wove through the commercial streets, we met a wave of encouragement from the crowds as they cheered and offered enthusiastic high fives.

It appeared there was an abundance of speed everywhere (not the rapidity in movement, but a more loose reference to the recreational drug). It was a surreal concoction of paisley, comical moustaches, sweet smelling pipe tobacco, plus four slacks, silk cravats and flat caps or the ubiquitous berets (c'mon, we were in the heart of France). Not forgetting the women, adorned in floral displays and vivid makeup. A spectacular portal of sixty+ years past had conveniently appeared gapingly in the dazzling surroundings of the Loire Valley. Everywhere compelled by fun and frivolity in the spirit of eccentricity and uniqueness. I felt like we had been transported back to when people had fun, or more fun than we appear to experience nowadays.

Bottle necks occurred on every substantial incline as a cavalcade of infrequent cyclists became a cavalcade of frequent walkers, but this only complemented the already laidback atmosphere. The event is extremely well organised, rest areas were dotted regularly along the route offering cake, fruit juices and much needed shade, as well as the occasional glass of wine. I chose to halt after experiencing the Robert & Marcel underground cellars at Saint-Cyr-en-Bourg, the dark dank surroundings eerily lit by the dim lights powered by the odd dynamo. As I departed I encountered a lavish vintage car traffic jam. I wove through the vehicles with ease, continuing my journey to Château de Brézé and lunch. The area is a pleasure to cycle with constant long meandering lanes and little hamlets, a perfect incarnation of a sublime rusticity.

I followed a stripy clad rider sat neatly atop a penny farthing into the stately grounds of the Château, and what an exquisite spot for lunch. As I sat devouring my elegant picnic we were entertained with a hypnotic repertoire from a group of musicians. The scene was one of eminent peace. Unfortunately, it was time to leave and I set off on what I thought was a continuation of the 55km route, but my propensity to get side-tracked had tellingly kicked in, and I got horribly lost and confused as I began to head back to Saumur, no longer on the correct route.

This was the least of my problems as my shifter cable snapped whilst attempting a moderate climb. After some advice and assistance from a resourceful Polish couple and a gang of locals, it was agreed the *vélo* was technically 'bust'. Thankfully, help arrived in the guise of a support van, the mechanic animatedly agreed with the diagnosis and provided me with an unwieldy replacement, a Ville d'Angers city bike (à la Boris bike).

Eventually, I found myself pedalling alongside a remarkably rotund and pleasant German, who gleefully informed me I was somehow 25km into the 55km route. His English was embarrassingly better than my English and we happily spent half an hour pedalling and chatting. The scenery was fine, wide open countryside brimming with millions of summer flowers covering the horizon in a spirited tapestry of colours. I found myself at the intriguing entrance to the extraordinary Perrières Cathedrals, a rousing amphitheatre of stone and troglodyte ingenuity. The site is known as the Doué-la-Fontaine and the experience was magical, the caves enhanced by strategically placed lights. I felt galvanised, but unfortunately as I appeared into the daylight, the rain was again persisting it down. I donned my rain jacket and pedalled on towards Chênehutte-Trèves-Cunault and the banks of the Loire. As I approached the bridge, which is an absorbing introduction to the town, I was astonished by the crowds all crammed onto the river banks. In need of refreshment, I paused for a delicious orange juice before following the contours of the Loire into Saumur and onto the finish line, which was enveloped with a swell of well-wishers applauding everyone through the 'Arrivée' sign.

With the cycling over, the rest of our stay was pre-occupied by pure decadence. That night we were treated to a magnificent meal within the walls of Fontevraud Abbey. A joyous mix of modern and ancient, ordered by atmospheric cloisters and simple chapels. It's an enigma, the surroundings so peaceful but equally so dramatic. It's bizarre to think it was once a prison, what a sirenic setting for confinement. At its peak, it was home to two thousand and seven hundred prisoners and said to be one of the harshest prisons in France. All throughout its history the Abbey has been intimidated by tyrannical individuals, from the Abbess to prison guards. I slept soundly after a late jaunt exploring the Abbey and its plethora of buildings, if you have an afternoon to spare, then I'd certainly recommend a visit.

Up early once more, our day commenced with a visit to Ackerman wines and its caves, eye-opening and innovative. The caves were originally created to source local stone, and this has left a stunning space which has been brilliantly put to use to host art exhibitions. The surroundings provide a showpiece for up and coming local artists to demonstrate their flair and imagination. As we wandered through the 'Voyage au Centre de la Bulle', the dark and damp setting was enhanced visually like a Christmas grotto, the bright vivid colours a brilliant concept, well executed. C'est très bien, Ackerman.

After a delicious lunch within a magically cramped, dimly lit troglodyte cave we ventured to a rose garden. The relaxed surroundings were a joy, the air scented dramatically with an effervescent floral bouquet. The garden was created in 1999 by the owner of the local zoo. The current owners took over in November 2013 and assure me that it is home to ten thousand flowers with nearly one thousand varieties of rose. The owner explained that the area is overwhelmed by rose production (half the roses in Europe are grown in the region) and they even provide the floral displays for the Anjou Vélo Vintage that adorn the watersides.

Next on our chaotic itinerary was the Château de Brissac, the tallest château in France. We were lucky enough to be introduced to the Marquis who was a genuinely decent chap. The château attracts 45,000 visitors each year and consists of seven floors. Our guide was extremely knowledgeable about the family and the building. From the château, we headed to our hotel for the night in Angers.

21 Foch is situated in the heart of the city and is a noble boutique hotel. The decoration is a mix of grey and white tones with a minimalist ambience and striking clean lines. Angers is an engaging place ordered by trams and pedestrianised streets with the most convivial locals. It's synonymous with its association with slate, even being referred to as 'The Capital of Slate'. The next morning we went off to explore with a local guide who explained the city is home to arguably the most absorbing museum in France, the Musée des Beaux-Arts d'Angers. The absorbing building is in fact made up of several buildings from different époques and displays a rich and varied collection of art works.

Our final destination was the city château, which was originally built as a fortress in a great defensive location. The highlight of any visit here is the 'Apocalypse Tapestry' which is housed in a museum within the château walls. The tapestry was commissioned in the fourteenth century and depicts the story of the apocalypse from the Book of Revelation on a series of six tapestries, reaching over 100m in length. It originally totalled ninety scenes but only seventy-one survive today. The colours of the threads are a mix of blues, reds and ivories with gilt and silver dextrously woven into the wool and silk. Nowadays the tapestry is surrounded with hi-tech lighting and ventilation systems to protect its integrity and beauty.

Amsterdam

Anjou Vélo Vintage

Ballyhoura Mountains

Birmingham

BMX, Perry Bar

CEMEX and road safety

Shanghai

Connemara

Coventry

Cricket Nights

Cycle Touring Festival

Dutch Press Awards

Edinburgh

Manchester

Mick Ives Racing

Monkey Boy on the South West coast

Giant's Causeway route

La Véloscénie

Po Valley

Prudential RideLondon

Rennes

Le Mans

Hastings

UCI Cyclocross, Milton Keynes

Utrecht

La Vélo Francette

Tour de Yorkshire and David Millar

Birmingham, a glorious verdant expanse in the second city (June 2014)

I have to be honest, Sutton Coldfield didn't stir my cycling imagination. The town is classed as a substantially wealthy suburb to the second city, Birmingham. This modern urbanised metropolis of chaos, people and motor cars would not be an automatic choice to pedal, but what I was about to discover would surprise and captivate me in equal measure. I love the fact that when you search for Sutton Coldfield on Google Maps, it's labelled as The Royal Town of Sutton Coldfield. How posh? I was about to find out.

The attraction wasn't immediate, a stereotype of an area surrounded with remnants of industry past and present. We were away for a weekend of glamping in the Boldmere area, so my plan was to immerse myself in the surroundings and enjoy the time on two wheels (making a concerted effort to banish any preconceptions and just simply pedal).

Our base was on the perimeter of Sutton Park close to the Powell's Pool reservoir. I will briefly explain, we were here for a Sea Cadet Regatta and would be camping with over three hundred, 12-18 year old cadets and the odd adult (Oh joy, I hear you say!). The predicted weather was positive and as we set off I still had to battle those pesky pre-conceptions, the image of a skyline with chimneys bellowing out smog.

I was surprised to discover that Sutton Park is the largest urban park in Europe and covers 970 hectares, attracting over two million visitors each year. It offers an array of attractions and the landscape is a mosaic of heathland, wetlands, marshes and seven lakes. We had arrived early evening; the sun was still happily dancing with a youthful exuberance. We pitched our palatial tent in close proximity to Powell's Pool, the venue for the weekend's watery fun and near the Boldmere Gate entrance to the park.

After a sweaty, fidgety night's sleep I appeared from the canvas to be greeted by bright uninterrupted blue skies. The temperature was already well established as I departed the campsite and I made a slight detour towards the water of Powell's Pool. Constructed in the 1700s, the dammed water was used to power a mill which was demolished in 1936. I was distracted by a substantial grey structure set back from the road, and encased behind metallic prison-like gates. Its appearance was imposing as the early morning sun created a crescendo of shadows. I later discovered that it's used as a Sea Cadet dry-docked training vessel called the Concrete Corvette. The building has been constructed to replicate a ship and doesn't disappoint, a perfect choice to identify the home of the Sutton Coldfield Sea Cadets.

As I negotiated the cattle grid at the Boldmere Gate and pedalled into the park, the horizon opened up to a verdant tapestry of colours and the comforting image of cattle and ponies happily grazing in their normal habitat. I was immediately surprised by the sense of wilderness and isolation that could be found within a well-established urbanised environment. The Boldmere gate obtained its name from Boldmoor lake situated nearby on the Chester Road and provides plenty of parking for any visitors.

There is a well organised network of paths and tracks throughout making it an ideal location to either cycle or walk. The roads within the park have a 'Heavily Restricted' status with the only access contained to traffic into and out of the park; any through traffic is completely blocked by the expert use of sturdy gates. The speed limit has been reduced significantly over the years and currently stands at a meandering 5mph. This is clearly great news for cyclists and walkers, who can enjoy the divine surroundings without the constant threat of pollution and noise whilst significantly reducing the impact on the road surfaces. Around the edges of the woodlands is a plethora of banks and ditches created to help protect the trees from the grazing animals. The whole experience is one of peace and relaxation.

The area is rich with history, there are the preserved remains of Icknield Street (a Roman road), an ancient well and several unassuming prehistoric burnt mounds. It began life as a Royal forest in the 9th century for the Anglo Saxon Kings of Mercia and by the early 12th century, it was a well-established deer park. In 1997, English Nature designated the park a National Nature Reserve and a Site of Special Scientific Interest (SSSI).

As I progressed further into the greenery, the road surface fluctuated between tarmac and light gravel, from which emanated a tantalising crunch beneath my skinny, rather exposed, tyres.

I had discovered from the always helpful and efficient Sustrans, that NCN 534 (also known as Plants Brook route) enters the park. The route is small, mainly off road, and follows Plants Brook from the Birmingham and Fazeley Canal near Minworth to Sutton Coldfield and then onto Sutton park when it eventually joins NCN 535.

I exited the park via the Streetly Gate and headed towards the city centre. My focus was the canal area in and around the ICC/NIA and Broad Street. Due to the time of day, the roads were relatively quiet and I made good progress. The surroundings changed quite significantly as I advanced, the horizon now dominated by grey drab tower blocks and urbanised gloom. Nevertheless, there was the occasional glimpse of wonder and artistic flair on an innocuous street light or building. Somehow I managed to find myself safely in the heart of the commercial area of Broad Street. The street is the dynamic heart of the city's nightlife with a glut of bars, restaurants and entertainment venues. Its evidently moved on since the 1700s when it was a simple un-named country path. I noticed running along the pavement, brass stars and the names of famous brummies. This is the 'Walk of Stars' a less glitzy alternative to the 'Hollywood Walk of Fame' and names included are Ozzy Osbourne, who was the first to be honoured in 2007, Jasper Carrott, Frank Skinner and many more. From this bustling thoroughfare, it was only a short pedal ride to the seclusion and serenity of the nearby canal.

I rested in the amiable surroundings of Cambrian Wharf, set just to the east of the NIA. I was astonished to find two people admirably tinkering with some bikes. Their base was a vibrantly decorated barge adorned with the ventures name, Cycle Chain. It's a not-for-personal-profit company with charitable objectives and simply refurbishes unwanted and unclaimed bikes for sale to the public. It was established in 2000 and has an ethos to work with people with visual and mental impairment, as well as those recovering from mental health problems, by providing training in bicycle maintenance and to promote cycling as a cheap and sustainable form of transport. The floor was dotted with a selection of tools and bikes either being stripped or lovingly re-furbished, after a brief chat I left to immerse in the Birmingham and Fazeley Canal.

From the wharf the canal descends quickly from the Farmers Bridge flight of locks, which a local animatedly informed me is an exhausting exercise. As I stood on the bridge, I couldn't fail to notice the iconic BT Tower protruding skywards. The city is slowly waking up to the fact that its network of canals is a huge environmental asset, and improvements and re-developments are happening all the time. This is in no small way thanks to the tireless work of the Birmingham Canal Navigation society, with its emphasis on restoration and promoting awareness.

The towpath was a constant flow of city dwellers, the area exuding a cosmopolitan feel. There were plenty of boats moored up, the occupants there to discover nearby Broad Street and the NIA. There is something special about the canals, especially if you travel along a city centre, the tranquil and calming atmosphere amidst the bustle of urban life is a reassuring breath of fresh air and provides a satisfying glimpse into the past.

Breeze, the initiative from British Cycling is gaining popularity across the UK (September 2014)

As the UK revels in the success of the Grand Depart, British Cycling's Breeze Network has revealed that participation in its female-friendly programme has increased by 32% year on year, engaging over fifty thousand women across the UK since its conception in 2011.

The announcement sees the women's initiative on track to help British Cycling reach its target to sign up one million women to cycling by 2020.

The latest British Cycling figures reveal that over five million women in the UK ride a bike and contribute around £50 million to the cycling economy. One million more women would like to take up cycling, but cite a fear of the roads and desire to find someone to ride with amongst the main deterrents to their participation.

Since its launch, Breeze has trained over one thousand women to become cycling champions – organising over ten thousand free rides for women in over two hundred and sixteen communities to get more confident and able on their bikes. The network has now introduced two new events – Breeze Challenge Events – for women wanting to train for a longer ride and progress their cycling ability.

British Olympian and Breeze ambassador, Emma Pooley, said of the increase in women's cycling participation: "It's fantastic to see so many women engaged with cycling. Though it was great to see so many people support riders in the Tour De France, the sport continues to be male-dominated and focused, so getting girls involved at grassroots and encouraging community women's cycling is so important".

"The Challenge Events are another example of how women's appetites for cycling is constantly on the increase and introducing these new rides is crucial to giving women a fresh and exciting new aim."

Stewart Kellett, Director of Recreation and Partnerships at British Cycling, said of the launch: "The challenge ride market is dominated by male riders and we want to use the Breeze Challenge Events to inspire more women to take up regular riding and provide a great experience for all participants."

"Through a combination of two great routes, fun events, two levels of challenge riding and a great day out for all involved in riding, supporting and spectating, Breeze Challenge Events will deliver the very best organised ride experience."

"With the ultimate aim of influencing and driving real change in the cycling market, we hope that more women go on to ride in many other challenge events once they build their confidence and fitness."

The introduction of Breeze Challenge Events is designed to be the next leg of the journey for many women who have developed their confidence and cycling skills through Breeze rides and are looking for an exciting new challenge to train and prepare for.

I was lucky enough to Interview Jess Varnish, British Cycling's most promising young talent and enthusiastic Breeze Ambassador.

In your role as an ambassador for Breeze, what do you think are the major challenges you face or will face?

I'm proud to be an ambassador for Breeze and champion women's cycling. I hope to help inspire and encourage more women to get involved with the programme and find their passion for the sport. I think the most significant challenge is bridging the gap between men and women participating at all levels, which is something that British Cycling have recognised and are working towards closing.

Why do you believe there has been a seismic shift in women participating in cycling since the inception of Breeze in 2011?

Ultimately because cycling is fun and programmes such as Breeze have made it more accessible in a way that allows women to enjoy riding their bikes. Breeze's success is having a huge impact and I'm sure it will continue to inspire more women to take to their bikes in the years to come.

How can you make cycling more attractive to women?

By breaking down barriers to participation, removing stereotypes and providing opportunities to get involved with all cycling disciplines at every level. British Cycling recognised the gender imbalance within the sport and launched their Women's Strategy in 2013, with a vision to inspire one million more women to get on bikes by 2020. The Breeze network is an integral programme to help achieve this vision, providing thousands of bike riding opportunities for women of all experience levels all year round.

Why do you think the figures for female cyclists in the UK is relatively low compared to their male counterparts?

The difference between the number of men and women cycling is not a new problem, but one that dates back decades, however, things are getting better. British Cycling's strategy to get a million more women cycling is going well with more opportunities being made available for women to get started in cycling, both in competitive events and more leisurely bike rides. The number of girls taking up the sport is huge too, so that gives us hope for the future!

Is it all about education and promoting from the grass roots?

Absolutely, education and training break down many barriers to participation, such as safety, by building cycle confidence, awareness and skill. Getting into cycling recreationally, with programmes like Breeze is a great way to find your love for the sport, in an environment where women can share information and experiences and develop their skills with help from trained Ride Leaders. That in turn can lead to progression in the sport, whether it be taking part in sportives, distance rides like Breeze Challenge Events, joining a club, or racing.

How much impact do you think having the Tour in the UK has had on encouraging non cyclists to jump on a bike?

I don't know if there are any statistics available as yet, but it's clear that loads more people are riding bikes. You just see people on bikes more now that you did five or ten years ago, and it's great to see! My only hope is that politicians take note and make the most of this opportunity to make cycling a great option for everyone by improving road conditions.

For the Breeze Challenge Event in October, what are you likely to encounter, if participating? Any tips?

Taking on the Breeze Challenge Events this October you're likely to encounter mixed weather, a few hills and the odd wobbly moment where you feel the burn. Having said that, you'll most definitely feel supported throughout, enjoy great camaraderie along the way and most importantly have fun from start to finish.

In terms of tips: train, and build up time in the saddle to prepare you to complete the distance. Breeze have designed special training plans to follow, also a number of the Breeze champions are organising training rides in the lead up that you can join. Be prepared for the day, get your bike serviced, make sure you take layers for all weather conditions, and fuel right, keep well hydrated and take plenty of snacks – a handful of jelly babies have saved many a cyclist.

What's next on the radar for yourself?

My focus first and foremost is on the British National Track Championships, and then it will be the track season which starts with the UCI Track World Cup in November. It's a big few months for me as we look to build up our training towards the World Championships and I'm looking forward to the challenge!

Po Valley, exploration by barge and bike. (May 2015)

Venice, a kingdom synonymous with water and in keeping with tradition, was to be both the starting point and, ultimately, the end of my exploration around the Po Valley. I had been invited by HF Holidays to experience one of their fully inclusive barge/bike trips.

After landing at Marco Polo airport, I had to make my way to Mantova, 120km west of Venice, so after several hot bus and train journeys I arrived in the bustling town. It was Saturday afternoon and as you would expect the centre was awash with bodies. The main part of the town was very pretty with an understated charm, and the ever-present ghosts of the Gonzagas family in the air. The city's central location and abundance of waterways has greatly developed its importance.

The boat was moored in Porto Catena, a lovely spot with sweeping views of the lake, it wasn't due to sail until Monday morning. After a rather fidgety sleep, and a healthy yoghurt fuelled breakfast, we were introduced to our bikes for the duration. More than adequate (probably would suit my mother), bright orange but sturdy enough. After a brief introduction from Hugo Gietelink, our Dutch guide with flowing grey hair and a distinctive El Capitano hat, who originated from Amsterdam and therefore happily allowed us to rib him constantly that Utrecht was a very beautiful city, we set off; our Italian journey was about to begin.

The group consisted of twenty-eight with a diverse range of nationalities, British, American, French and surprisingly the majority from Australia. Most were retirement age or older but all were keen to explore and discover the beautiful surroundings. We were being hosted by Ricardo, the captain, Erika, Silvia and Giovanni on board the glamorous boat 'Ave Maria'. To refer to it as a barge would be understating its imposing structure; it has twenty rooms and plenty of space to accommodate comfortably a mass of sweaty bodies, especially after a long day in the saddle.

Mantova is a simply beautiful Renaissance city with a cavalcade of history, an abundance of towers, battlements, churches, cupolas and an intricate network of atmospheric alleyways. There is a stunning collection of palaces and the town is best known for its numerous squares, Piazza Sordello, Piazza Broletto and Piazza Erbe. Its population is four hundred and fifteen thousand, which is above the national average and it sits at the south-easterly tip of the Lombardy region. Thankfully the environment is completely flat, with only some occasional soft hills.

The whole area is dominated by water, especially the Po, with an extensive capillary network of canals, inland lakes and wide lagoons. The lakes were created in the twelfth century by the architect Alberto Pitentino to protect the city from flooding. The construction of a system of dams and locks led to a useful and dramatic inclusion to the environment.

To accompany your trip, you are given your own personal 'Green' bike guides. The set is presented in its own rather fetching handlebar case and consists of a booklet with detailed maps of the itinerary: in colour and scaled 1:75,000/50,000, a roadbook with detailed description, stage by stage of the itinerary with precise directions and a travel guide with all the expected important information of the history and heritage of the places you will visit. HF Holidays make it easy even if you would prefer to take on the Self-Guided option, they are so proud of this material they constantly update and fine-tune the information. Bravo!

Day 1 – Mantova Long Round Trip

Exploration of the lakes 40km and no elevation sounds simple enough. We departed Porto Catena after a lazy breakfast, the weather was glorious. We initially followed the contours of the Lago Inferiore through some beautiful tree cover, thankfully the entire Mantova – Venice route is marked by yellow arrows. We halted briefly as we departed onto the roadway by the monument to Martiri di Belifore (Martyrs of Belifore) which was erected to commemorate the patriots of the Italian Risorgimento who were executed between 1851 and 1855 on these very shores. The memorial was wonderfully imposing, its clean lines cutting sharply into the bright blue skyline. The pedalling was sedentary and everybody appeared comfortable with the pace. After approximately ten kilometres, we stopped in bustling Curtatone, the market was in full flow, the area dominated by a rather animated lady on a microphone. She became even more excited when she noticed our mass of bikes. The town is famous for its magnificent church, the Santuario delle Grazie (Sanctuary to Our Lady of Grace). A visit is highly recommended, it's recognised as one of the most important places of pilgrimage to the Virgin Mary. The interior is bizarrely macabre but so hypnotic; the darkness is dominated by stucco and shells, with the elevated gallery containing a selection of life size figures representing the miracle that saved their life. Oh, not forgetting the chained, stuffed crocodile hanging from the ceiling, its role to act as some form of talisman to ward of evil spirits. See I told you bizarre!

After a coffee stop we continued onwards, our next goal was the Museo Etnografico dei Mestieri del Fiume di Rivalta, which tells the story of river, its flora, fauna and the basic relationship between man and river. It afforded a wonderful collection of tools and equipment and I found it refreshing that it was all in Italian; they had not made the effort to convert the displays into English. It was only a short pedal push to our lunch stop in Laghi di Mantova where we all descended on a sleepy Trattoria. An hour later we were heading back towards the boat, the sun was still as strong and our water consumption was considerable. The boat was a welcome sight, we had explored plenty and already friendships were being made.

Day 2 – Mantova to Zelo

We docked at Governolo, one of the largest inland basins in Italy, the small town lies on the stunning Mincio River. One of the largest systems of river locks in Italy is situated here to balance the different water levels of the Po and Mincio. We followed a dyke (there is a joke there!) for the majority of the day. The weather was glorious, strong sunshine with a hypnotic headwind, we made good pace, the group happily pedalling past several substantial locks through Ostiglia (famed for its medieval fortress and floating mill).

We stopped in the beautiful Revere; a small town which is often overlooked, it has a population of two thousand, five hundred people but possesses so many hidden charms, again dominated by the legacy of the Gonzaga family. The approach to the town was stunning as we pedalled on an elevated section of grassy bank with the Po on our right and red tiled roofs on our left. The town once possessed an entire substantial fortification; unfortunately this is no longer visible apart from the imposing bell tower. As we departed we stumbled on a rather surreal war memorial, a steel creation of barbed wire, a soldier in repose and the memory of the lives lost across generic wars. From Revere, our next stop was Bergantino, the town is famous for the creation of fairground rides, our group treated themselves to a visit to a museum dedicated to the great fun of the fair. The exhibition is set-up to create the atmosphere of the simple fairground with an ornate collection of wooden horses, pipes, musical devices, billboards. We even managed to dance whilst listening to the Italian national anthem. Some of us (Hugo) displayed a creative flair as a bizarre mix of foxtrots and rumbas dominated our surroundings, I wasn't sure what the poor guide felt about the experience, befuddlement and amusement were definitely appropriate.

From Bergantino we continued to move sedately towards the cheese factory Caseificio Sociale Ballottara, it specialises in making Grana Padano. The landscape was a collection of rolling pastures and placid arable farmland. We had a tour of the factory, which was most welcome as the shade was a much needed distraction, however the smell of the stacked cheeses was very overpowering.

Our day ended in Zelo, again a small town but with plenty of character, we made an adventurous foray in the darkness to the local cemetery, the tombs evocatively lit, creating a stunning sombre light show. The tranquility and experience was mesmerising. The night ended in the local bar listening to Jim expertly strumming his guitar.

Day 3 – Zelo to Adria

I decided to experience the boat for the day, it's not a pre-requisite to pedal so on this occasion several of the group decided not to get on the bike. The sedentary life of the boat as it negotiated the locks and waterways was a compelling draw. The slow pace was rather infectious, it promoted a lethargic approach to life, providing time to contemplate our simple existence, if life is in fact that simple, mine especially. The scenery was glorious, a mass of greenery from the endless cavalcade of flourishing embankments. We ended the day in Adria nestled between the Adige and Po rivers; with a population of twenty thousand, it was once an important trade centre along the navigable branch of the Po. Its attraction to visitors is the diverse architecture with remnants of the Greeks, Etruscans and Romans.

Day 4 – Porto Viro to Chioggia

Boat, sleep, write, boat. I had to keep up with my writing so I experienced another peaceful day on the water. We eventually docked in Chioggia; its stunning location on the southern edge of the lagoon of Venice was breathtaking. I went off to explore, I had to negotiate a plethora of fishing boats and the rather pungent fish market, it obviously still had a working relationship with water, birds were swooping down to see if they could scavenge some lunch. As I encountered the main road into town, I noticed the attractive architecture; unfortunately the rain was now incessant. The place was dominated by locals on bikes, all ages happily weaving through the narrow streets. The town is sometimes referred to as 'Little Venice' and you can immediately see why, with it being constructed on an island and interlaced by canals which are crossed by ornate arched stone bridges and mainly untouched by the effects of mass tourism. The main artery is the Corso del Popolo which is a lovely avenue with a wide pedestrian area, dotted with plenty of shops, restaurants and cafes with tables invading the pavements. I stumbled upon the Chiesa di Sant' Andrea, the church has a beautiful marble façade and is home to a magnificent Crucifixion by Palma il Vecchio (1480-1528). I paused for several minutes, to remember my loved ones. The majority of the buildings have porticos as imposing features and these cannot be found in any other lagoon towns or cities.

Day 5 – Chioggia to Venice

This was a simply stunning stage following the thin strip of land that separates the Venice lagoon from the Adriatic Sea. The ride was a mix of inviting sandy beaches and fine views of the lagoon. On 4 November 1966, a high tide measuring 194cm submerged Venice, Chioggia and many other surrounding areas. So it was decided to create a special law to plan interventions to prevent a re-occurrence and the MOSE project was created and eventually there will be a collection of seventy-eight mobile dams to protect the harbours and lido. Work began in 2003 and is planned for completion in 2016. The transportation system is extremely efficient; the water-taxis are reliable and relatively cheap.

Venice happily combines an aura of calm juxtaposed between the chaos of thousands of tourists and the demands of religion. It's easy to be mesmerised by the world famous architecture, I explored the narrow side streets and alleys, the ever changing pace of life was an unexpected revelation. I stopped on several occasions and was taken aback by the total solitude before turning a corner, there to be confronted by a throng of people who were conversing noisily. All these streets and alleys appear to terminate at St Mark's Square, which is an ideal location for strolling, pausing and contemplating. A wonderful pavement café ambience dominates, however the prices might not be to your liking. I ambled contentedly.

In conclusion, this was a wonderful adventure with great people, great accommodation, great gastronomy and great laughs. The itinerary was easily manageable by all abilities and Hugo (guide) was a mine of information, his animated and enthusiastic explanations were a delight. The climate in the Po Delta is ideal for exploration by bike, being very hot and humid in the summer, with no distinct rainy months, but it does tend to rain more in the autumn and spring months. I travelled in the middle of May and the first part of the week was extremely hot with the second part rather rainy, like you need more water in Venice! With a cavalcade of history and culture dominated by the ruling dynasties of the Este and Gonzaga families and the crowning glory, the lagoon and the sea, this was a completely unforgettable experience and one I will always remember fondly, especially Hugo getting lost and trying to cover his tracks by introducing us to the cows, explaining that they produced *milk*! Hilarious!

Manchester, an underbelly of cycling history (September 2014)

It all started with a simple correspondence about a cycling exhibition being held at the Museum of Science and Industry (MOSI) in Manchester. From that email it quickly became apparent that there is a deeply ingrained legacy of cycling and bicycles within the city. The Pedal Power exhibition marks the twentieth anniversary of the opening of the National Cycling Centre in the city, the home of British Cycling.

The itinerary as usual was noticeably chaotic which I've come to like and expect. Meet Sustrans, explore Pedal Power, pedal around the Velodrome, crash a Team GB training session and finally visit another cycle exhibition in nearby Rochdale, and all this in only three days. I couldn't wait. The strong association that the city has with cycling wasn't clear to me prior to my trip, but what I was to discover is a city that is completely comfortable with the bicycle and proud of its connection with all things two wheeled.

After alighting the train and hurriedly depositing my bag at the hotel, I was ready to meet Sarah Roe from Sustrans. She is the North West Regional Press Officer, her passion for her role in the charity and cycling in and around the city was immediately apparent. The plan was to discover the city on two wheels after catching up with Peter Green, Area Manager for Greater Manchester and unmistakably a keen cyclist. He had planned to join us on the ride but was recovering from a cycling injury, so frustratingly had to decline. Immediately I felt at home on my bike, the roads busy but not hazardous.

First port of call was the Takk café, an Icelandic inspired artisan coffee shop in the quiet tranquil side streets of the Northern Quarter and a meeting with the charity's top man in the city. Sustrans have spent a lot of time promoting Manchester and its surrounds as a great, safe place to cycle. Peter's enthusiasm and passion were apparent and although he acknowledges that the city's cycling journey is still in its infancy he has clear and dynamic plans - one is a designated safe cycle route through the Rusholme area with the introduction of (armadillo) traffic segregation initiatives. They provide a low cost way of reallocating road space and have been trialled in Salford with mixed reviews. He was also positive about the Fallowfield Loop, Sustrans flagship route. It provides an easy off road and secure convenient route to a selection of local schools; nevertheless he is aware that they need to generate funds to keep standards high, with maintenance of underground structures and tree growth being key areas. He states it's all about education and local communities taking on-board the whole cycling ethos, and acknowledges it's not all about the bike, but about the community. The major aim is for ten per cent of all journeys to be made by bike by 2025. As part of the plans they are working with a number of organisations within Manchester on the new 'Bicycle Account' which uses the model taken by Copenhagen, where they regularly report on all aspects of cycling provisions and work to improve them. Manchester is one of six cities in the UK in the Bicycle Account.

Galvanised by our coffee stop, we said farewell to Peter and set off from Great Ancoats Street along the bramble-lined Ashton Canal towpath. I always adore the canal especially in the city, the escapism and tranquil confines provide a literal breath of fresh air. The route took us past some contemporary apartment buildings, and turned out to be a great alternative, less frenetic route to access Sportcity and the Velodrome. There are plans to upgrade this as a part of the Cycle City Ambition Grant to be delivered by Transport for Greater Manchester, Tameside Borough Council, Canal and Rivers Trust and Sustrans, with completion expected 2015. The majority of the route is well maintained and gloriously green. From Sportcity the route continued along the in-filled Stockport Branch Canal before we found ourselves pedalling on the old disused Fallowfield railway. The occasional cyclist or jogger was our only company. At eight miles, the loop is thought to be the longest urban cycleway in Britain and is a haven for hikers and bikers with a wealth of tidy, well signposted trails. The route is owned and managed by Sustrans whose role is to monitor and protect wildlife on the trail.

We moved to the road network in the pretty confines of Chorlton. Sarah explained the area is favoured by workers from the nearby BBC. It's popular with trendy young professionals boasting a selection of independent shops, bars and restaurants. Almost immediately I was taken aback by the whole simple rusticity of the surroundings. I had read that a newsagent on the main street reputedly sells more Guardians than any other shop outside of London. Pure decadence in the suburbs of Manchester, it's every bit as delightful as it sounds.

The plan was to meet David Barker, a volunteer ranger on the Trans-Pennine Way at Stretford. The route is twenty-five years old and David was instrumental in its creation and is currently a Group Co-ordinator on the Manchester/Trafford section. The popular leisure route runs coast to coast between Southport and Hornsea, with the section between Manchester and Liverpool very popular. He explained his role involved predominately looking after signage, vegetation encroachment and bridge diversions. He also enjoys the weekly Monday rides which usually take about two hours. The tranquillity was astonishing especially considering the A56 was nearby and would no doubt be busy. Reassuringly the route was a constant flow of riders wearing big grins as they whizzed by. We followed David deep into the vegetation and virile tree cover, along a network of dusty gravel tracks, as he guided us back towards Chorlton Water Park. The surroundings a stimulating mix of green hues and bucolic sun shaded charm.

We neglected the canal on the way back and followed the roadway. I think Sarah wanted me to experience 'first hand' the attractions of Rusholme, affectionately known as 'The Curry Mile'. Sustrans has recognised the need for more defined designated cycle space along this road. The route was at times precarious but considering it was rush hour (and one of the busiest bus routes in Europe) the traffic didn't seem to impact on our pedalling too much. There were several hair-raising moments and vigilance is indeed an essential facet.

Our last stop of the day was back in the city at the hospitable 'Popup Bikes'. The business is set within old railway arches and offers an original place to enjoy a coffee after a long ride or just simply store your bike for the day. The ethos is simple, 'to put community before profits' which is commendable. The open airy space is a great place to meet friends or just linger over a cappuccino whilst your bike is being repaired. A visit is highly recommended, actually I strongly advise you experience the friendly unhurried service, you won't be disappointed.

The next day I had another packed schedule. My first destination was the MOSI – Museum of Science and Industry which was only a short pedal ride from the hotel. Manchester's affiliation with cycling has its roots in the very earliest days of the sport. To mark this twentieth anniversary, and pay homage to the city's longstanding cycling heritage - the Museum of Science & Industry proudly presents Pedal Power. This brand new and family friendly exhibition opened in July and celebrates and explores Manchester's rich cycling heritage past and present. It runs until 1 March 2015 and is open daily.

I was here to discover the exhibition which is housed in the small and atmospheric Highlights Gallery within the Museum's Station Building, this intimate space is the ideal setting to fully showcase and immerse visitors into the world of cycling. Focusing also on the track, the technology and the teamwork that has contributed and evolved over the years. I was unaware of the affiliation the city has with cycling before my visit and was shown round by Curator of Industrial Heritage at the Museum of Science & Industry, Meg McHugh, who explained:

"The Museum has a significant collection of bicycles - so this exhibition provides an ideal opportunity to really show them off. With the Tour de France kicking off in Yorkshire a couple of weeks before Pedal Power opened, and just a few days ahead of the Commonwealth Games in Glasgow, it was such a great time to really instil in a new and future generation of cyclists and riders that Manchester, in particular, has contributed so much over the years to Britain's love and success in this fantastic sport."

They are especially proud of the acquisition of the exact bike Victoria Pendleton rode to glory at the London and Beijing Olympics. Although, the highlight for me was the paraphernalia once owned and won by Britain's first cycling mega-star – the Bury born and bred Reg Harris, especially his flimsy helmet and ballet looking shoes. As an amateur he won two Olympic silver medals – whilst recovering from two broken vertebrae. He went on to win the world professional sprint title four times as well as Sports Personality of the Year twice. It was great to see these exhibits which were previously hidden away. My competitive nature was adequately satisfied as I pitted myself against Olympic greats on the interactive time trial bike. I was proud of my performance (albeit I might have underestimated the distance) until Meg had great gratification informing me that a local fifteen year old lad had crushed my time recently by several seconds. Thanks Meg!

From the Museum I was directed expertly by Rachel (Senior MOSI Press Officer) to the National Cycling Centre. It had been arranged for me to have a taster session on the track. Even though the directions were comprehensive, I still managed to get lost (don't tell Rachel). Eventually, I arrived with the aid of some helpful local security guards. The building has a contemporary facade and as I walked into the cafe, I nearly literally bumped into Laura Trott and Joanne Rowsell. The whole place was a sea of red and blue British cycling kit.

The taster session was a great experience, initially terrifying but mostly exhilarating. You are given a pair of clip shoes and a helmet and then ushered off to change (me in my long heavy fabric shorts, not ideal). As you step out into the velodrome, the silence is surprising, the space is spectacularly surreal. The walls bank quite steeply, team GB tandem were on the track when I arrived and they were seriously licking some speed. I wasn't sure I'd be going as quickly or adeptly. The National Cycling Centre was Britain's first indoor Olympic standard cycling track, and since it opened in 1994, is one of the World's finest and fastest indoor tracks. One lap is 250 metres, and the banking's are 42 ½ degrees.

After safety advice I was let loose onto the blue sedate part of the track, the instructor clearly wanted to see how confident and comfortable I was on the bike. Plainly reassured (rather remarkably), he told me to move up the track as I gradually gained momentum. It was a weird sensation as I ventured further up the banking, remembering to keep a constant pace to prevent a calamitous crash. It was bizarre to think that I was following in the pedal pushes of countless Olympians. You are required to pedal continuously, unfortunately I have noticed I tend to freewheel in my day to day riding but you couldn't do this on the track bikes. The further I went, the more confident I became until I was pedalling at the giddy heights of the top of the wall. Unsurprisingly it's an energetic sort of place, a controlled chaos dominates. Almost everywhere you look there is something of its rich history to be seen. Once you have successfully completed a taster session and are eager to progress further, the track programme provides a structured pathway to enhance your track skills and fitness. Once the session was complete I had the opportunity to sit and watch Team GB put the track through its paces. Hereafter, the effortless pedalling and sleek, athletic, professional attire of the Pros was more than a match for my performance or shoddy appearance I had demonstrated only a few minutes earlier.

My final day was spent in Rochdale at the Pioneer Museum. 'Co-operation on Wheels' is a special exhibition looking at how bikes were used by Co-operative societies and members, how and why the Co-operative Wholesale Society manufactured bikes and how a new wave of Co-operatives are keeping the historic links alive. It runs until 1 November 2014. As I approached the building I was immediately drawn to the groovy new interactive cycle sculpture stood proudly to attention outside. The funky and contemporary design spells out the word 'Coop' and fires the imagination with its vivid interpretations of the hills synonymous with Rochdale, the town hall and a selection of colourful bikes. The sculptor Richard Dawson worked with local children to create the piece and it's a great showcase to what lies within.

I met with Jennifer Mabbott, the Museum Manager, she explained that several Co-operatives sponsor Tour De France teams and the exhibition explores a new wave of Co-operatives that are keeping the historic links between cycling and Co-operation alive! The exhibition is an interactive joy with the Tour de France theme running throughout, you can design your own Tour de France jersey, play a cycling wheel of fortune game, and have a chance to win a bike courtesy of Edinburgh Bicycle Co-operative. My favourite story was about a bike that was left at Bradford train station in 1947. It had been purchased by the Bradford Co-op but nobody collected it so it sat at the station for decades before being bought by a member of the public, who donated it to the museum. The whole experience was truly captivating, just like my time spent in this part of the North West.

Cemex, making great strides in road safety (March 2015)

At the recent London Bike Show I had a really interesting conversation with Elizabeth Young from Cemex who, as an organisation, are actively researching additional safety features for LGV's. They see this as an important factor especially bearing in mind three cyclists have been killed in London involving Large Goods Vehicles (LGV's) already during 2015. At the show they were inviting cyclists to get into the cab of an LGV, done in conjunction with the Met police, to demonstrate the blind area around these large vehicles. Currently a lot of work is being done on additional safety features for LGV's, such as 360° cameras, etc., and, in addition, an alternative approach - research and development on vehicle design. On my return home, Elizabeth contacted me again and invited me to a briefing, which included the opportunity to go out in one of their vehicles so that I could experience for myself the vehicle interactions on London's busy roads from a driver's perspective. She assured me that to go out into London during the rush hour and interact with traffic is quite an 'eye opener'. I have to admit I was intrigued so I arranged a visit to see for myself.

Cemex is one of the country's biggest cement producers with over three thousand employees (which amounts to approximately six million hours worked) across over four hundred manufacturing sites in the UK. These sites are serviced by a fleet of nine hundred vehicles which cover over thirty-nine million miles each year (which I am reliably informed, can sometimes get you to Mars!). For over fifteen years, the company has recognised that road safety (especially incidents involving cyclists) is a high priority and they have spent plenty of time and money in researching and developing new processes and systems to reduce the impact of their vehicles on the British roadways. So with that in mind I was up early, initially utilising the tube, then the overground, before arriving in Westholme Park where Elizabeth (Liz) picked me up and drove me to their Asgain site. The expected hustle and bustle was immediately evident, an array of LGV movements tormented the horizon, the noise was tremendous, the blur of Hi-Vis paraphernalia demonstrating the over-arching importance of safety. After a Health & Safety Induction and provision of some fetching Personal Protective Equipment, it was time to meet my driver and my guide for the duration, Andy.

He was a rather affable chap and, after acquiring his load and checking the correct weight on the weigh-bridge, we set off; our destination was Fulham, some sixteen miles across the City. He happily informed the journey would take around two to two and half hours ('What, to cover sixteen miles?' was my surprised response). We immediately hit traffic and this continued throughout our journey. Andy methodically explained all the safety features on the vehicle, consisting of side mirrors, mirror for front of the vehicle, sensors on the left of the vehicle which operated whenever the vehicle was close to something on its nearside, and a camera which was continually recording everything that happened within the cab. Which we both agreed was a good inclusion, but acknowledged that it could be a drivers 'Best Friend' or 'Worst Enemy'.

Cemex have been leaders in the implementation of safety systems for many years and have understood that these systems needed to evolve through time. Pre 2000 their vehicles had been installed with reversing bleepers and cameras, between 2001-2004 they rolled out nationally cycle signs and blind spot mirrors Class V1. Side scan was installed between 2004-2007 and tipper guards followed 2007-2012. A complete safety review was carried out in 2012 and, finally, camera trials took place in the same year. Cemex still continue to be pioneers in this area and they will shortly be trialling some new vehicles with glass bottomed nearside doors, so that the driver can see cyclists/pedestrians without the aid of any other safety features (but in-conjunction with them) to make the vehicles even safer.

As we progressed across the city it became evident that Andy's main frustration was with the lack of the cyclists wearing any Hi-Vis attire or equipment. It is not hard to disagree with him, most cyclists are happy to pay the price of a second hand car for a bike so why is it they are unable to find a few quid to purchase a Hi-Vis gilet.

As we continued, it was noticeable that the lack of visibility was not just concentrated to cyclists, a large quantity of motorcyclists also seemed oblivious to its benefits.

Andy continued to become frustrated by the attire of the cyclists, many in business suits, no helmets and sometimes bizarrely just luminous gloves, the gloves evoked a mix of annoyance and hilarity and I could see why. If you have actively recognised that Hi-Vis has to be a consideration, why then would you decide to adorn the smallest and possibly the most expensive form of PPE? Now I too was getting frustrated!

To be honest the antics of the cyclists didn't come as any surprise, as Andy was eager to point out in his own formidably articulate manner. "Look at those idiots on the pavement", "Did you see that cyclists behind us run the red light?" but he was equal in praise when he felt it was required. "Look at those two, they have come past me and stayed in the cycle box in front", "Excellent, the lady on the racer has passed me on the right."

Nonetheless, he will admit that the majority of cyclists we encountered that day adhered to proper road etiquette, as did the majority of the other road users. Unfortunately as our lengthy journey continued we both had to agree that there are good and bad drivers – and cyclists – and the only way to move forward, is to educate. How this is best achieved is a question for another day but I can personally attest to the advances that Cemex are making to ensure our streets are safe for all road users. I commend them for their efforts, they have gone above and beyond, and will continue to lead and push for more robust legislation.

With the likes of Andy, and many others like him on their payroll, their efforts will not be wasted, his enthusiasm and dedication will without doubt save countless lives as he continues to make his slow way through the streets of the Capital and Kent. I don my hat to you, fella, you are a credit to your employers and, if any cyclists out there encounter a Cemex vehicle on your ride, I suggest you show them some appreciation because through their efforts and commitment, your cycle home is, and will continue to be, safer than ever before. Thank you Cemex and finally to Andy, please try not to get too frustrated by the lack of Hi-Vis or helmets as we cyclists are a strange breed and like to be individual, which unfortunately means we like to decide what is safe, no matter what research or guidance might say.

La Véloscénie (September 2014)

I finally arrived in Alençon, in the early evening, after the confusion of one way streets and lack of signage. I had a room booked at the Hotel des Ducs, directly opposite the train station. What a room, contemporary, minimalistic and extremely spacious.

I met Carole from the Orne tourist office and we went off to discuss the itinerary over dinner. She explained I would be following the Véloscénie on gentle gradients which seamlessly connect Notre-Dame de Paris to Mont Saint-Michel, it crosses four regions, eight counties, two National Parks and five UNESCO World Heritage sites. I was already sold on the idea before I had finished my delicious starter.

The route is 434km long with over 130km on signed and secured voie vertes (greenways) and 200km of shared paths with little or no traffic. www.veloscenie.com. Carole was enthusiastic about the joys of cycling and detailed animatedly the type of terrain I would encounter, sweeping valleys, plenty of forests and quiet rustic lanes. I was in for a treat.

Next morning I was up later than usual, a peek through the curtains was accompanied by a depressing sigh, as the weather was gloomy. After re-packing my now substantially weighted rucksack, I set off declining the lure of a bizarrely English breakfast. I pedalled into the heart of the City, stopping briefly by the Basilique Notre-Dame. Its ornate, surreal façade dominates the surroundings, it was destroyed in 1744 and partially rebuilt in two different architectural styles. The absorbing religious iconography on the exterior is exquisitely carved and lifelike, especially the gargoyles, it provides a tantalising glimpse into the past.

The D204 was relatively busy as I departed Alençon en route to Carrouges. The sun was now happily dancing and I was confident of my orientation (I had been given a Vélo guide which was sturdy, informative with detailed maps and, considering it was in French, it was a great addition to my already hefty backpack). The route re-kindled my relationship with a sublime rusticity, the country lanes absolutely deserted with no signs of life. The only sound was the faint clunk as my pedals revolved at a moderate pace which allowed me to immerse in the scenery.

I arrived in Carrouges as lunch was being taken, the commercial streets empty, the bars and restaurants consumed by a noisy hilarity. I didn't want to miss out, so I took a seat at a popular restaurant and ordered the Plat de Jour, which was, peculiarly, an Italian dish. Over coffee I caught up with the itinerary, a large part of the afternoon had been set aside for a visit to the Château with which the town is synonymous. Suitably refreshed I set off to find the historic residence.

Carrouges Château is tantalisingly visible from the heart of the town. It stands imposingly in the distance at the end of a gradual descent, the gatehouse tower is absolutely mesmerising and is considered to be the first sign of Renaissance architecture in Normandy. This brick, granite and slate Château remained in the same family from the 14th century until 1936. The surroundings are breathtaking, efficiently manicured and lovingly maintained. I was shown round by a jovial guide, who explained that the courtyard is the best place to see the different stages of construction, from the fourteenth century keep and the fifteenth century Blosset wing which still possess three of its original features, with the highlight being the Gothic chimney stack. It's a great place to explore, loads of rooms stacked with period furniture and art, I especially liked the Louis XI bedroom, the king stayed here in 1473.

A short distance from Carrouges, I arrived in the small village of Sainte Marguerite de Carrouges and the cider farm of L'Aunay et Hugues and Corinne Desfrieches which was my base for the night. The welcome was warm and the room was substantial, on the site they make cider and other apple based alcohol beverages. I was given a brief tour by the owner Hugues, his passion and commitment to all things apple was immediately evident. After a brief rest it was time for dinner. I was lucky enough to be invited to eat with the family, what an honour. The food was delicious, the conversation was a mix of broken English and broken French but we managed to converse about everything, from politics, to family, sports and distinctly cycling. After dinner we moved from the kitchen table to the football table, the whole family competed in a somewhat competitive and noisy match. After an abysmal showing, I said my farewells and retired for the evening with the jubilant expression of the young son firmly planted in my head; I should for a fact stick to cycling.

The next morning as I took coffee, I witnessed the magnificence of nature as the sun and the mist created a mind-blowing display over the manicured orchards. I headed back into Carrouges and breezed past the Château, the surroundings conquered by luscious greenery. The unequivocal solitude was simply prophetic and I moved sedately through the dramatic tree cover. Kilometre by verdant kilometre I was introduced to an inspiring and fantastical landscape. Small cultivated plots brimming with energetic colours were being tended lovingly by locals. The Véloscénie signs were frequent, enabling me to orientate with only the occasional glance at the map or guide.

Bagnoles-de-l'Orne is a remarkable place, it curiously promotes an overwhelming feeling of wellbeing. Its location enveloped around a monopolising lake and nestled deep in the vast Forêt des Andaines, only adds to its appeal. I stopped by the ornate fountain to survey the surroundings; there were plenty of cafés, gastro restaurants and artisan regional shops bustling with life and providing a notable confusion. My hotel was in a great spot with heart-stirring views of the water. The Hotel Beryl is equipped with a heated indoor swimming pool, a spa and beauty therapies. The décor is modestly contemporary, the rooms spacious and inviting.

After checking in, I went off to explore. The spa town has been frequented since the end of the seventeenth century, but its fame only spread at the end of the nineteenth century. It's a magnet for those wishing to escape the monotony of daily life and pamper themselves. La Belle Époque quarter is the highlight and is situated on an area of forty-five hectares and comprises of three parallel boulevards, four streets and a central square. The buildings simple construction are undermined by the flamboyant multi-coloured façades, exquisite works of art using basic sandstone and brick as a surreal canvas. The four colours used represent blue for water, green for the forest, yellow for the air and red for the earth.

After a substantial lunch, provided by Restaurant O'Gayot, I liaised with Carole from the local tourist office. She provided me with a hand held audio commentary so I could experience the Discovery Trail – a great journey to the heart of the town. The trail features twenty stages and exposed me to the raw history of the town using the architecture, geology, history and some bizarre anecdotes. Even the relatively scary looking mushroom family adorning the signs to aid orientation didn't put me off, as I explored every nook and cranny with vigour and a childlike enthusiasm.

That evening I had yet another delicious gastronomy experience courtesy of the hotel, before retiring to my substantial balcony to enjoy the night-time lightshow of the bustling resort. A great day in a great place.

I explored the banks of the lake and its well-maintained gardens after breakfast. The sun was already shimmering off the placid waters, I departed the town on the D335 before reverting to another voie verte in the heart of the forest. I halted in the deserted Perrou, the weather began to change and I was tormented by dark ominous clouds and a decrease in temperature. I pushed on in the hope of avoiding any downpours. After a short period listening to Coldplay, and ferociously pedalling, I arrived in the outskirts of Domfront.

Domfront is accepted as 'Les Plus Beaux Détours de France' ('The Loveliest Detours of France') which is a list of a hundred towns from two thousand to twenty thousand inhabitants that is recognised as being of outstanding character and located off the beaten track, usually featuring exceptional heritage sites or listed monuments. Its scenic charms are well known.

I pedalled into the Cité Médiévale, this old centre is beset by vibrantly decorated timber-framed buildings, labyrinthine cobbled streets and beautiful townhouses. Originally the city ramparts were protected by twenty-four towers, although only eleven survive today. I stopped by L'Église St Julien in need of a rest. Stepping inside, the church appears casually dark, the atmosphere was lifted as the sun illuminated the strategically placed windows. The interior of the church is gripping, the decoration is neo-byzantine and the highlight is the magnificent Christ in Majesty in the semi-circular chancel.

The town sets a fairytale scene, medieval flags hanging from timber buildings, cobbled streets without any cars. It would have been more appropriate to see a knight on horseback than a Renault or Citroën. I made my way nonchalantly towards the tourist office, I had a meeting with Eric who would show me the hidden charms of this special place. As we wandered around the castle grounds he illustrated quite vividly the reasons for the castles construction, as a defence along the Normandy border, strategically placed overlooking the Varenne, it controlled the road from Caen to the province of Maine and the county of Anjou. Much of the original castle is now in ruins having been deliberately demolished in 1610. Its mildly dilapidated state is alluring and the vestiges of the stone keep set a dramatic backdrop to the pleasing gardens.

After lunch I was again pedalling on an engrossing voie vertes in the direction of Flers, this 20 km route follows an old railway line and contours the banks of the river Varenne. I had left the Véloscénie behind and was now on the V43 which runs for 615km between Ouistreham and La Rochelle. The landscape fluctuated between shaded foliage and open farmland, it was idyllic. In no time at all I was pedalling on the roadway into urban surroundings of Flers. The horizon was influenced by ominous dark grey clouds, I halted briefly by a Turkish bar and whilst sipping a drink, the heavens finally opened with an enthusiastic onslaught. The downpour appeared set in for the day and unfortunately I had a meeting with a local taxi driver in the nearby village of Fumencon several kilometres away. So, in a display of British resolve, I stepped out into the incessant rain and pedalled onwards, following the voie verte signs into Fumencon and the welcoming vision of a warm and dry motor vehicle, my transport back to civilisation. Shame!

Who says Milton Keynes isn't interesting. (September 2014)

On Saturday 29 November, 2014, for the first time in history, a round of the UCI Cyclocross World Cup will take place outside of mainland Europe. Milton Keynes hosts the best riders from around the globe. The event is sponsored by Trek and the hope is to enhance brand emphasis in the UK, especially with the general growth already in cycling.

"We are very excited to welcome Trek on board as a major partner of the Milton Keynes World Cup," said Event Director Simon Burney. "Trek have stepped up to be a leading player in cyclocross, supporting both teams and events, and their partnership with us at their home town World Cup will I'm sure give Katie Compton and Sven Nys added motivation; hopefully, they will still be able to concentrate as they pass around the course-side Trek VIP area, where support for them will be huge and very loud! In year one, we are very proud to be working with Trek and grateful for their expertise and support."

The UCI Cyclo-cross World Cup is a season-long competition organised by the Union Cycliste Internationale (UCI). First held in the 1993–1994 season, there are currently four editions, tailored to the different categories of riders: elite men, U23 men, junior men and elite women. In brief Cyclo-cross is a form of racing which usually takes place in the autumn and winter (the international or "World Cup" season is October–February), and consists of many laps of a short (2.5–3.5km or 1.5–2 mile) course featuring pavement, wooded trails, grass, steep hills and obstacles, requiring the rider to quickly dismount, carry the bike while navigating the obstruction and remount. Races for senior categories are generally between thirty minutes and an hour long, with the distance varying depending on the ground conditions. The emphasis is on the rider's aerobic endurance and bike handling skills. It all sounded like some mucky mayhem and I couldn't wait.

I arrived early afternoon, the sun was an appreciated guest and the subsequent temperature was mild for the time of year. The place was a buzz of excitement, absorbed by a mix of (carelessly grating) cow bells and animated commentary over a PA system. My first observation was the whole place was a massive quagmire. OK, I am not that naïve or ignorant to not expect a muddy and boggy course, but this was the spectator's area! I even, at times, struggled to ensure my unsuitable footwear (trainers!) remained on my feet and not in the gloopy swathe of mud. On reflection it was great messy fun and I briefly felt like a child once more!

The Women's Elite race had just finished, as I approached the finish line, and had been won by Sanne Cant (Enertherm-BKCP) after a close finish from Katherine Compton (Trek Cyclocross Collective). British rider Nikki Harris (Young Telenet-Fidea) was third some distant from the leading pack. European and Belgian champion Cant took the World Cup leader's jersey, holding a sixteen point lead over Pan-American and US champion Compton. As the mud encrusted riders rapidly left the track I noticed to my astonishment the makeup of the crowd, it was influenced by families all adorning beaming smiles, woolly hats and those pesky cowbells (not forgetting the occasional dog)!

There was now a lull in proceedings before the main event, the Mens Elite race so I made my way to high ground to survey the course from a great elevated position. The size of the course was astonishing, the route (and the crowds) snaked through Campbell Park in a controlled chaos. Big screens eclipsed the horizon, beaming re-runs of the Women's race; the whole atmosphere was one of a collective joy and patient anticipation. After exploring the Media Centre and VIP tent (where I bumped into one of my writers tucking into a free lunch, no names but you know who you are) and partaking of several lukewarm coffees, it was time to immerse in all things Cyclo-cross. The crowds were six deep all around the course; the excitement was electric as the race began in a crescendo of enthusiastic cheers, cow bells and the commentator over-describing every action in real-time. As I walked around the track there was a collective frenzy, the noise levels were at fever pitch, the burger vans were doing a roaring trade, satisfying the crowds with their usual unhealthy but tasty fare, and the beer tents were practically busting at the proverbial seams. It was just a great place to be!

As the race progressed and the surface deteriorated the fun and drama began, especially on the downhill sections and sharp corners. The spectators treated to skids, unseated mud-splattered riders, and a rugged demonstration of strength and tactical ability from the competitors. The pace was intense with the riders displaying a simple but assured confidence whilst skillfully manoeuvring their bikes around the muddy track. The concentration and commitment was visible on every riders face as they battled resolutely the worsening conditions. My adrenalin was pumping so I can't imagine what emotions the riders were experiencing.

The bikes were taking a battering, their quirky design with a lightweight but sturdy aluminium frame pure cross and the hike-a-bike-friendly cable routing, which reduces the effects on cable contamination from the mud and dirt, is a common and a definite necessity. The major differences between the two are the frame geometry, and the wider clearances that cyclocross bikes have for their larger tyres, which were working overtime this afternoon.

As the race neared its conclusion, the excitement and noise increased significantly, a constant fervour and anticipation was overwhelming, and this was transferred to the track. The ferocious enthusiasm of the commentator on the loud PA system only added to the overall experience, as they described a blow-by-blow account of the dramatic finish. Kevin Pauwels (Sunweb - Napoleon Games Cycling Team) outsprinted his teammate Klaas Vantornout to win. The pair made it out of the mud and onto the paved section together before Pauwels showed greater strength to pull away and increase his lead in the overall World Cup standings from Vantornout. French Champion Francis Mourey (FDJ.fr) outmuscled Lars van der Haar (Giant-Shimano Development Team) for third place. On reflection, I was exposed to a riot of mud, more mud, excitement, apprehension and simple fun. The event offers a great family spectacle of cycling. The pace is intense, the strength and tactical ability of the riders is thrilling, they exude a quiet re-assured confidence. The demonstration of fortitude and basic resilience is commendable and makes this a momentous cycling event and so easy to recommend to the masses. Let's hope the UCI recognise the success of the Milton Keynes event and make it a permanent fixture on their World Cup calendar, it truly deserves it!

Women's Evening at the Bikeyard, making cycling attractive to all (December 2014)

I am a passionate fella. I adore my family, I adore my wife and I adore my bikes. This passion extends to promoting the benefits of pedalling, the physical qualities are universally recognised but the mental well-being is as much a key factor and not always noticeable. I had recently interviewed Jess Varnish about her role as a Breeze Ambassador and was intrigued by the passion she enthused about women's cycling and decided that the topic should have a voice, an outlet to encourage more ladies to hop on a bike and enjoy the many positives of two wheeled transportation.

My first task was to commission my non-cycling other half to spend more time (in fact, just *any* time), in the saddle and pen some words with the hope of making it a regular feature, thankfully she obliged. So with this in mind, I was more than fascinated by an email I received one humdrum afternoon. A colourful poster appeared in my inbox advertising a Women's Cycling Evening at a bike shop conveniently in my hometown, with the offer for me to attend. The chance to champion women's cycling and promote my local community was too much to ignore, so I responded with a resounding 'yes, why not'!

Unfortunately, due to my now chaos-filled schedule and a bout of Man-Flu, I didn't get to the evening but still felt it warranted some exposure, especially as there has been a seismic movement in the amount of women participating in cycling in the UK. The plan was to interview the organiser of the event, Michelle Paget from the Bike Yard, a popular bike shop in the heart of Royal Leamington Spa. So on a sufficiently miserable rain affected day I arrived with two children in tow, the lure of shiny bikes had been enough to convince them the visit was a good idea. (Oh, not forgetting the promise of some sweets!)

The shop is a kaleidoscope of vivid colour brimming with all manner of cycling paraphernalia. I was met by the smiling, slight oily face of Michelle, she had clearly been tinkering out the back, of course I immediately liked this lady.

What inspired you to organise the Women's Evening at the Bikeyard?

Working every day in the shop I often get female customers asking questions regarding how to best look after their bikes, this sparked me to create a workshop maintenance evening that would provide the ladies with an opportunity to learn more about how to look after their bikes. I wanted to give these ladies as much info as possible in order to keep them cycling and thought that it would be a fantastic opportunity to not only give them maintenance advice, but advice on all things concerning female cycling. Bringing together brands, influential guest speakers/riders and information for them to take with them. Getting all the ladies together and offering info and advice in one evening.

Was there a good turnout?

I was totally blown away by the amount of ladies that we had through the door in one evening. Approximately seventy ladies came. It was really nice to see and feel the buzz within the shop celebrating all things concerning female cycling and so many different areas of cycling too. From Downhill to Road it was so good to see. I was also blown away by the support from the companies and guest speakers/riders. It felt really good being supported by so many female friendly distributors and supporters.

Are you going to make this a regular event?

From the success of the first event we definitely intend to re-run the event in the spring, I am also arranging a regular maintenance evening slot for ladies too.

Why do you think there has been a significant increase in women's cycling in the last couple of years?

Women's participation in cycling, I believe, has grown massively in the last couple of years, due to influential female role models that are not only racing or riding for themselves each week but supporting women's cycling as a whole by backing supported rides and opportunities to encourage more women on bikes. With support from British Cycling with the Breeze network and female specific training and events, I believe it makes a massive difference. This not only gives women encouragement to participate in a relaxed and non-pressured environment but also introduces them to more cycling avenues for the long term. Having a female rider to aspire to, whether its Laura Trott on TV competing or a seasoned fellow club rider that rides week in week out, I feel that women do tend to support and encourage each other a lot and this leads to more females on bikes, supported by each other.

Do you regularly cycle; is it for fitness or convenience?

Hell, yeah! I cycle as much as I can and whenever I can. I cycle to work most days (which isn't very far) I regularly ride MTB trails at weekends, sometimes local routes around where I live or perhaps travelling a little further afield to trail centres and well known riding spots. I also like to participate in off road events. Off road marathons and the odd XC race event also. I am even contemplating an MTB 4x event this weekend coming – AGGGHHHH!! Hang on and howl. I cycle for pleasure and it definitely does give me a lot of pleasure as I really do love my bike.

What bike do you normally ride?

Currently, I have two bikes. I mostly ride "Arnie," my beloved MTB XC bike Giant Anthem – awesome bike, always a pleasure to go out and ride this one, seriously I really do love this bike! qnd, of course, there is "Charly," my other lovely bike, a single speed MTB/4X bike that was created from parts and brilliant to blast around on. However in the pipeline is a CX bike but it's still on order, once it arrives I plan to give some cyclocross a go.

What other 'Women only 'activities do you offer at the Bikeyard?

Trailtakeover - As a keen mountain biker I helped set up and run #trailtakeover – female only MTB rides which originated from local rides at the bikeyard. Trailtakeover now takes place in various locations and this year we not only met at four different trail centres but we also offered a local 50k off road challenge that started at the bikeyard and took us around some of the local trails. www.trailtakeover.com

Breeze - Volunteering as a Breeze ride champion I hold regular rides from the bikeyard. We just completed a ride on the 16th November that was available on the women's evening for ladies to sign up to. We had a good turnout and attracted some new-to-riding riders, so that's another box ticked for me.

RLS Cycling Club –the bikeyard is founder and sponsor of the local club RLS Cycling Club. I am a qualified level 2 cycle coach for the club and I have planned some women only cycling coaching sessions. In these sessions I plan to introduce the ladies, who are completely new to cycling, to gain skills that will help them ride on the roads confidently. These sessions will take place in the New Year and details are here www.rlscyclingclub.com.

Do you think the Cycle Industry is catering adequately to women?

I think that within the last couple of years the industry has definitely become more "female" friendly. I think that the growing numbers of female cyclists has forced companies to sit up and take note that not only are we around, but growing in numbers. The companies are starting to create female specific ranges with women in mind. With lots of manufacturers now employing female engineers and designers, the bikes, products and clothing ranges are not just made pink and smaller, but perform effectively to suit a women's shape and riding set up and are also more appealing to the female market.

Are there any specific types of cycling (road, MTB, touring) that your female clients appear more interested in?

Road cycling is undoubtedly the most popular of all the disciplines. I would estimate that over half of the sales to women are for road or road fitness cycling. Close second I would say is Hybrid/Fitness bikes and sadly followed by the MTB's (need to steer more ladies to the muddy side of cycling).

In your opinion, what do you think attracts women to cycling and is it sustainable?

I think that more and more ladies are becoming attracted to cycling as a form of staying fit and in shape. The other attraction I believe is that, whether its road or MTB cycling, it can be very social and enjoyable with friends, which makes it appeal to an even wider female audience. I often have ladies come into the shop to buy an entry level bike thinking they will not use it or like it so much, these ladies usually return when they realise they are hooked and want to upgrade. It's awesome to see this, and every single time a new bike is released I feel a buzz inside knowing that yet another female cyclist is heading out to embark on her riding experiences.

The glorious North Coast of Ireland and the captivating route of the Giant's Causeway Sportive (April 2015)

This was my first trip to Northern Ireland, for once I had no pre-conception, ok, just one. I had heard so much, read so much, people just simply pontificate about the geological and mystical presence of the Giant's Causeway. The phenomenon is immediately recognised worldwide so a visit was not to be missed!

My first task after escaping the airport was to pick up a bike from Chain Reaction Cycles in the city before heading west towards Ballycastle and my temporary base. I arrived in Ballycastle around lunchtime, the attentive receptionist told me I could not check-in until three p.m., so there was only one thing to do: get out on two wheels. The temperature was warm, the sun was shining, the normally efficient Carol Kirkwood had got it wrong for once.

My trip had been arranged by the helpful Beverley Pierson from Outdoor Recreation NI, she had sent me a couple of OS NI Discoverer series in the post. Conveniently, she had marked the routes of the sportive on the map with strategic points. I am a passionate advocate of a map, the tactile, tolerable, musty smell is one of its major attractions.

As I left Ballycastle, I was presented with a steep climb; the route was well signed and brown in colour as expected. As I climbed, the tops of the mundane buildings were replaced by a magnificent azure horizon and sweeping vertiginous landscapes. It reminded me of a less weather beaten Isle of Wight. The coastline of any country is always one of the most evocative locations that any place can be rightly proud of and the Giant's Causeway route doesn't disappoint. The road was well surfaced and the scenery picture card quality. My positive outlook enabled me to pedal at a relatively quick rate and I halted briefly by the entrance to the Rope Bridge at Carrick-a-rede. All the locals rave about the Rope Bridge.

I continued eastwards, the roads were still quiet, I deviated off the main road in the direction of the harbour at Ballintoy, the grass verges overflowing with cars, it was unmistakably time for church. There were several sharp bends to negotiate as I descended towards sea level. The roads were narrow and thankfully I didn't encounter any other vehicles. The Harbour car park was relatively empty, the views were beautiful, the rain had stopped and a chink of blue was trying its best to protrude through the clouds. I was treated to an absolutely striking panoramic view of White Park Bay, the bay is guarded at one end by Gid Point and Long Gilbert at the other. The blonde expanse of the beach was completely deserted, the sea was a noteworthy blue. After I over-snapped in a childish enthusiasm, I located the Causeway Road, the Giant's Causeway couldn't be too far away now.

Dunseverick Castle is only a few miles from the Giant's Causeway, its flippant, desolated image, is in fact its attraction. The location is surreal set amongst a collection of bungalows and I stood, completely engrossed in the simple surroundings. It was a unique discovery. It was only a short pedal from the Castle to the Giant's Causeway, the roadway was poor, plenty of potholes to keep the cyclist occupied (which was a shame, considering it's on the approach to a World Heritage Site). The car park was overflowing with a mass of coaches, mini-buses and cars – no sign of any other bikes. My photographer for this trip was supposed to be my wife, Sarah, unfortunately circumstances dictated that she would be unable to attend. On her 'bucket list' is to visit the Giant's Causeway so I made a decision to not go in, I wanted to visit the heritage site as a couple. AHHH! But selfishly it would give me a reason to return! Logic in my madness.

From the Causeway, I headed inland towards Bushmills (yes Bushmills is a town and not just a brand of whiskey). In no time at all, I had arrived.

Bushmills is a normal rural town but with one worldwide attraction, the Old Bushmills Distillery. The visitors centre is well presented, a tour costs £8 for an adult. The factory is the only distillers of the drink in the world, the tour takes you through all the processes in the production of the much sort after beverage. The acquisition of the malt, the fermentation, the distilling and then the bottling processes are delivered in a memorable way so that all can understand. Our group consisted of an eclectic mix of nations and characters, the majority Irish but there was a hint of French and a single Englishman holding up the rear. We happily chatted about everything whiskey.

The Marine Hotel, Ballycastle, is a worthy spot on the seafront. The décor and welcome were exemplary, the rooms are of a high standard, clean and spacious and my stay was most definitely going to be fuss-free, relaxed and pleasant. My first meal was conveniently at the hotel restaurant, the surroundings were lovely, a lively receptive atmosphere. My starter was simple but very delicious, my opinion is if someone can perfect the simple things, then the more complex things will be easy. The Marine's food is a credit to the chef, it's well presented, tasty and accompanied with a plethora of industrious staff.

The next morning I was presented with a gloomy drizzle, so after a hearty breakfast my enthusiasm had increased somewhat. After sleeping with the map, I had decided to pedal east towards the Ballypatrick Forest (which in reality is opposite to the route taken on the Easy Street section of the Giant's Causeway Sportive and allows the less able to miss out Torr Head), into Cushendun before heading north along the coast toward Torr Head and then back to Ballycastle. The gloom had now disappeared and had been replaced by a ghostly mist as I entered the peaceful surroundings of Ballypatrick, it was mesmerising. 'Scooby Doo, where are you?' was more than appropriate to break the silence. The surroundings were striking, I pedalled at ease, the route undulating through a collection of animated colours. After I had breezed past a windswept Lough (Lake), the landscape changed to a more barren, more desolate environment. The horizon bossed by noisy sheep and not much else. I was enjoying the tranquillity before I interacted with a somewhat impatient van (white, I hate to stereotype), all kids please turn away now! I decided to hog the road in a remarkably obstructive and childish manner which as you imagine tempered his enthusiasm (rage!), after a brief Tom/Jerry or Wile E. Coyote/Roadrunner moment, I eventually came to my senses, pulled over and as he passed, I proudly displayed my middle finger in praise of his exemplary driving. The simple things in life are free and always so satisfying.

Next stop was Cushendun, what can I say about Cushendun? It was nice enough but not exceptional, I stopped, chatted to several locals, most were complaining about the fact you have to pay to see the Giant's Causeway, whereas five or six years ago it was free, it appeared to leave a bitter taste every-time I mentioned it. It was bizarre because they all preferred the Rope Bridge, I visited neither but normally the locals are right! From Cushendun, I headed north along the dramatic coastline in the direction of Torr Head. As I climbed, visibility was non-existent, there were occasions when I felt I was completely pedalling into the unknown, I would imagine the best way to get your bearings is by scaling the Torr Head and being exposed to some far-reaching views. No chance today!

As I continued to climb, the hillside sketched out before me, before I arrived at the giddy heights of Torr Head. There was a mystical stillness in the air, the views of the Mull of Kintyre are usually superb so I halted only briefly before heading back towards Ballycastle.

Utrecht, The Tour de France comes to the Netherlands.
(April 2015)

Following a successful trip to Amsterdam last year, I had been invited back to the Netherlands and Utrecht which is the venue for this year's Grand Depart of the Tour de France. The glaring attraction for me was the Tour but I was also hoping to immerse in this historical city. Stena Line were happy to provide me with similar hospitality which as always was superb and as our ferry departed Harwich, my mind wandered, was Utrecht going to live up to my expectations? Plenty of people had raved about its qualities, I didn't want to be disappointed, but I was brought back to reality with the arrival of my delicious starter. Another Dutch adventure had begun!

We were staying on the outskirts of the city at the modern Postillion Hotel in the Bunnik area. The rooms were very much Ikea-esque, but comfortable, and not too far out of the city centre to give us a transportation headache. The city is home to approximately 330,000 residents but, with a massive 70,500 students utilising the services of the best university in the Netherlands, it's definitely a youthful, exuberant place to be. The city was only twenty minutes by bus (Bus No. 41) or 30/35 minutes by bike, path-side red and white signs display location names, the networks simple and clear design signage prevents any confusion and ensures you arrive at your desired destination with minimal inconvenience.

Lunch provided by the De Rechtbank immersed us to a delicious assortment of typical Dutch fare. The sumptuous 'nooner' was as much a treat on the eyes as it was on the palette. I was reliably informed, by the attentive waiter, that the 'soup, veal croquette, filet american, egg salad, green salad with parma ham concoction' was a type of Dutch tapas. It was bursting with a taste of Utrecht; enhanced by the modern and cordial surroundings, it was a gastronomic joy.

Utrecht is without doubt a bike city, the bike is absolutely everywhere, no lamp-post, railing or tree are left bike-less. Every day, between seven a.m. and seven p.m., over 100,000 cyclists ride to work, school, university, public transport, shops or home via the city centre. The city is even endeavouring to make cycling even more attractive, with the bike given precedence in the mobility policy of the municipality in Utrecht. The astonishing amount of bikes utilising the designated 'Bike Parking' places near the Central Station currently stands at 12,000 but the hope is to increase this to 33,000 by 2020. The construction of bicycle tunnels and fly-overs displays the commitment by the city to provide a convenient, safer alternative to the motor vehicle. They lead by example and the UK definitely need to take note and put proposals in place to match this forward thinking approach to cycling.

Our first task after a hearty (local) lunch was to meet our guide for a small portion of the afternoon, Iris. The weather was wet, but being staunchly British, I idiotically refused to don any wet weather gear. Iris was a wealth of knowledge, possessing a noble sense of humour and delivery, she explained the local history in a manner that ignited extraordinarily vivid images of the past. As we explored, the weather improved, the occasional chink of blue sky replaced the gloom. The time flew, as we listened intently to her perfect English, she exposed us to the unique canal system with its medieval wharves pinpointing out an unexpected 'hidden' world in unhurried surroundings, just a short distance from the main thoroughfares, the switch of emphasis from the hustle and bustle above was superbly indulgent. We were both intrigued by the steam rising in a theatrical but ominous fashion from sections of the roadway. Iris explained this hallucinogenic image was in fact modern art created to identify the location of the Rhine which was re-located many centuries previously. Unfortunately, our cultural jaunt had come to an end and we departed by the Dom-Under on the historic Domplein, the dramatic next stop on the itinerary. The Domplein is the city's epicentre, with a lively mix of locals and tourists all around. Since 2014, the Dom-Under has provided visitors with an insight into 2,000 years of the city, as you descend into the darkness you are presented with a fascinating underground amphitheatre. After selecting a large torch, you are free to wander and explore the relics from the Romanesque cathedral, churches and the remains of the Gothic cathedral which was left in tatters following a tornado in 1674. It was great adventurous fun, for a brief moment, I felt like a child once more.

An early night was required; plenty of fresh, if a little damp, air and an interrupted night's sleep on the water had eventually taken its toll.

The next morning I met my cycling guide, Edwin as the rain conveniently arrived, we decided to use a couple of the hotel's basic (but more than adequate) stash of bikes. He explained we would be following a part of the tourist route (interestingly devised by himself for Toerisme Utrecht) and the majority of the route of the TDF Prologue, with frequent forays onto the 2nd stages ride, which depart Utrecht to finish 166km later in Neeltje Jans in the province of Zeeland. As we departed the rain ceased, maybe we were in for a dry couple of hours. It will be the sixth time that the Tour has begun in the

Netherlands (Amsterdam 1954, Scheveningen 1973, Leiden 1978, Den Bosch 1996 and Rotterdam 2010) and will transform Utrecht into the cycling heart of the country with the world's eyes concentrated on how it delivers. The individual Time Trial (or Prologue/1st Stage) begins on the 4th July and for 13.7KM the riders will speed through the heart of the city. The riders follow a flat trail from west to east, beginning at the back end of the Jaarbeurs (the heart of the financial and commercial centre), they then head for the Galgenwaard Stadium (home of FC Utrecht), briefly encountering the entrance to the colourful Science Park, before a sharp bend takes them back westwards in the direction of the historic centre and the finish line on the Croeselaan. It sounds simple!

The tourist route took us away from urban surroundings and into the stately tree cover of the Amelisweerd, where we stopped for a coffee in the idyllic surroundings of the fairytale Theehuis Rhijnauwen. After a brief rest, we continued to follow the tourist route, dissecting the greenery en route to the city. We halted briefly by the Fort Rhijnauwen which was built in the nineteenth century as part of the New Dutch Waterline; unfortunately, only a small proportion of its structure is visible from the cycle route. We moved sedately through the campus of the vivid Science Park, with its buildings by celebrated international architects like Rem Koolhaas, Eric Egeratt and Wiel Arets; this was our first interaction with the Prologue route.

Edwin was desperate to show me the city's most famous architectural masterpiece, the Rietveld Schröder House which was nearby. Once again, my pre-conceptions were blown away, as I was expecting a medieval structure but the house was confusingly modern. As Edwin explained the background of the house, it became quickly apparent why this house was added to the UNESCO World Heritage List in 2000. Built in 1924 by Dutch architect Gerrit Rietveld, this revolutionary structure for the time is known worldwide as the highlight of 'De Stijl' and is visited by thousands from all across the globe.

It was now only a short pedal into the heart of the city, enroute Edwin proudly introduced the separate bike, car and bus bridge which has stood in the city for many years. The bus section is part of the Prologue route, this fact evidently made him even more proud of his adopted city, judging by the grin. Another detour found us on Maliebaan, which is believed to have been the origins of London's Pall Mall. The tree-lined boulevard appears to be just a normal straight road seen in the majority of towns and cities across the world. It holds a wealth of historic prominence. Hidden amongst the greenery was a house in which the first Dutch Cycling Association, the Nederlandsche Vélocipèdisten-Bond, was founded in 1883 and it's believed was the location of the first designated cycle path in the Netherlands. On that historic cycle note, we pushed on; as the crazy preparations for 'Kings Day' began, the occasional fancy dress costume struggling to pedal through the traffic.

Eventually, we arrived in the medieval heartbeat of the city, the Domplein. Everywhere, construction was taking place, re-surfacing roadways, re-generating buildings, re-inventing opinions, this is what the TDF evokes, a pride and passion in local issues and local community, hopefully this legacy will continue long after the star-studded peloton has ridden off south in the direction of Zeeland. The highlight was pedalling along the cobbles towards the Dom Tower, knowing that, in just over a month's time, the likes of Valverde, Contador and Froome (to name just a few) would have to also negotiate the same magnificent route.

Edwin deposited me at my next port of call, The Dom Tower (Domtrum) which on Stage 2 of the TDF will see the riders pass through its magical medieval arch, albeit in the neutralised area due to the cobbles and narrow streets and lanes, it will make a provocative addition to this illustrious race. It's an ideal setting for strolling, pausing and contemplating. The tower is the world famous symbol of Utrecht, the six hundred year old structure is the tallest medieval tower in the Netherlands. Climbing the four hundred and sixty-five steps (it's not as bad as it sounds) rewards you with an electrifying vista of the city, the totally different perspective to street level is astonishing. I descended with some moderate speed as I was conscious we had an appointment at the Het Spoorwegmuseum (the Railway Museum).

The Museum had decided to showcase Dutch Tour de France history, the exhibition titled "It's a long way to Paris – Dutchmen in the Tour" has been granted exclusive access to use archives and exhibits from a collection held at the House of Cycling Museum, with railway carriages utilised to display the illustrious array of bikes, jerseys and pictures of the Dutch athletes who have participated in the Tour since its inception. There is plenty on offer for all ages, with a bit of pedalling, if you so desire, especially the chance to experience the bumpy ride afforded by the cobbles of the Paris-Roubaix. The subtle but effective use of sound and imagery provides a shining tribute to the Dutchmen who have experienced the highs and lows of this world famous race and would appeal to all cycling aficionados (and evidently train buffs). The exhibition runs until 26th July 2015.

A dinner had been arranged at Humphreys, the restaurant is located in the historical city wharves at the ancient channel under the town hall. Wow, astonishing, speechless, unexpected, mesmerising are all adequate descriptions as you enter this underworld of gastronomic splendour. The décor is wonderfully ostentatious, with simple exposed brickwork arches, sitting comfortably with an orchard of glistening chandeliers and walls splashed in an understated 'boudoir' red. Did I already use 'wow'? The highlight of the three courses was the mixed grill, I suggest you remove the stereotypical 'British' image and replace it with a more refined minimalistic approach. A plate conquered by a trio of meats (chicken, pork and beef) adjoined in neighbourly harmony by a simple skewer and surrounded by a colourful array of greenery.

After dinner we were introduced to a feast of orange, its was the start of the 'Kings Day' festivities. We quickly learnt the Dutch can definitely celebrate, the centre was awash with makeshift bars, temporary stages brimming with bands, boats overwhelmed by reasonably inebriated locals and a garish, noisy hilarity, but the pace was still surprisingly sedate. It's a great city to explore at night, you can follow artistically lit locations throughout the historical city centre. Walking the 'Trajectum Lumen' route is a marvel, as the historic city centre is the backdrop to theatrical light art.

Utrecht has been in the shadows of Amsterdam for far too long, it is superbly compact, easily discovered by foot and even easier by bike, with perhaps a sweaty brow. It's a titillating mix of chic restaurants, auspicious cafés and a bubbling underbelly of artistic flair. A collection of pretty narrow cobbled streets and alleyways radiate towards the Oudegracht, the main waterway which hides a treasure trove of charismatic wharf cellars running along the towpath. The city is happily juxtaposed between the modern and the ancient, with plenty of Roman remains, the medieval wharfs, the gothic Dom Tower (the image that most hold in their minds eye when they think of the city) and the architectural modernity of high-profile designers, like Rietveld, Schroderhuis and the buildings of the Science Park. It's conveniently located, making it easily accessible by all manner of transportation, so why wouldn't you want to venture to the inspirational destination of Utrecht, it's a recipe for magical exploration.

How the legacy of the Tour is thriving in Yorkshire and I chat frankly with David Millar.
(March 2015)

The whole adventure began under a veil of mystery and the ubiquitous cloak and dagger. I had received an innocuous email inviting me to an event by a PR company working on behalf of a high-end car manufacturer (details top secret) to launch their involvement in the cycling arena, especially the up and coming Tour de Yorkshire. Intriguingly as part of this unveiling was the opportunity to ride with their ambassador David Millar, followed by lunch with David and then the chance of interviewing the former Pro. Unfortunately, they would not divulge who the car manufacturer was. It was all mysterious and somewhat intriguing, like a novel written by Ian Fleming. I was hoping that this secretive company would turn out to be Aston Martin, c'mon how brilliant would that be?

After a wait of several days, more information filtered through and finally the name was revealed, Maserati. The luxury Italian car manufacturer was launching Maserati Cycling, an initiative designed to celebrate the brand's new connection with the sport and to offer a series of new experiences for road cyclists. The rapid growth of road cycling in the UK has been particularly evident amongst Maserati customers and employees, whose passion for performance, sporting excellence and design provides a natural conduit to the sport. Like cycling, the Maserati brand has a rich heritage, and shares a reverence for history in its pursuit of engineering innovation.

Co-incidentally, I had also been approached by the nice people of English Country Cottages, who had kindly offered one of their high class properties to accommodate me whilst in God's Own Country. They have a selection of self-catering cottages conveniently in and around the route of the inaugural Tour de Yorkshire. Our base was at the Coach House in the lovely unspoilt village of Askham Bryan it was central to most things, importantly York was only five miles east.

As we approached the house, I was mesmerised by its exterior, it was a sublime feast of stone, the interior a modern interpretation of a traditional cottage. A mix of lavish spaces accessorised to the highest standard. The décor is clean, fresh and comforting and every detail is exquisite, from a welcome note accompanied by a beautiful arrangement of pink tulips to an array of colourful accessories with splashes of colour lifting each room. The owners are visibly proud of their property and it shows; they have sourced the most coveted items meticulously utilising an array of British designer Cath Kidston's sparkling accessories and the result is warming country elegance. There is an abundance of 'Mod Cons', several TV's, WiFi, radio and plenty of well presented bathrooms and showers. All the rooms are cosy and overflowing with literature and all manner of games to occupy all ages.

Outside, the garden is attractive, with a manicured lawn and a seating area ideal as a sun trap. There is plenty of parking and the house and village are strategically placed for a foray to York or further afield.

I had a free day before the hectic itinerary of the Maserati launch, so we ventured to the nearby historic city of York. Everywhere there are reminders of the Tour de France in the guise of yellow painted bikes. The Tour de Yorkshire takes place 1 to 3 May 2015; the route was recently unveiled in Bridlington, the town where the race will start. Ben Swift, Team Sky pro rider, and Brian Robinson, the first British man to win a stage of the Tour de France, were in Bridlington to celebrate the international cycle race, a direct legacy of the 2014 Yorkshire Grand Départ. The race has three stages and includes a women's event on 2 May, a mass participation sportive on 3 May, and a cultural festival.

Stage one, on Friday 1 May, will start in the seaside town of Bridlington and 174km later finish further up the coast in Scarborough. Stage two, on Saturday 2 May, is one for the sprinters, and will see the race start outside the imposing Selby Abbey. The route takes in much of the Wolds, and from Selby will take the peloton towards Market Weighton, through North Newbald and on to Beverley, where they will turn north to Malton, then on to Stamford Bridge. Spectators will have the chance to see a circuit of York and organisers are hoping for a dramatic finish in the town, which of course witnessed incredible scenes during the 2014 Grand Départ.

As part of the legacy of the Tour de France to get more women cycling there will also be a dedicated women's event on a circuit through York.

The final day, Sunday 3rd May will see the peloton make a return to some of the roads raced in the 2014 Yorkshire Grand Départ of the Tour de France, only with a twist; starting in Wakefield, riders will travel south to Barnsley before heading to Holmfirth where they pick up the Grand Départ route in reverse, racing to Ripponden before riding the iconic Cragg Vale – which in the Tour de France was the country's longest continual climb and now becomes the longest continual descent.

The race will be shown live on television in the UK and across Europe and a huge television audience is expected, once again shining a spotlight on Yorkshire.

The race is being organised by Welcome to Yorkshire and Amaury Sport Organisation (A.S.O.), with support from British Cycling and local authorities throughout the county, especially the start and finish towns and cities; Bridlington, Leeds, Scarborough, Selby, Wakefield, York and North Yorkshire County Council and East Riding Council.

Christian Prudhomme, Director of the Tour de France at A.S.O., said; "After the grandest of Grand Départs of the Tour de France, we were keen to return to Yorkshire. With its stirring landscapes, iconic cities and tough climbs, Yorkshire offers all the ingredients needed for a great cycling race. The welcome we received in Yorkshire in July 2014 was simply spectacular and I am very much looking forward to returning there in May for the Tour de Yorkshire".

York is a beautifully understated city and, best of all, it's captivated by the bike. Everywhere you look, the bike is invariably present, its approach to cycling appears similar to Oxford, the bike is the King, long live the King. The main roads are busy but, once you venture into the side streets, like the Shambles and around the Cathedral, it is a cyclist's delight; the locals are receptive to all things two-wheeled.

Maserati recognise cycling as a progressive market and are more than happy to be a major sponsor for the Tour de Yorkshire. Peter Denton, Region Manager for Maserati North Europe comments: "The sport is highly contagious. We have seen an ever-increasing number of our dealership network and their customers get bitten by the cycling bug over recent years. The excitement generated nationally by last year's Grand Départ was mirrored across our team and network, so the

Tour de Yorkshire legacy event provides a suitably high profile ride with which to kick off our two-wheeled activity."

For Maserati and its customers, at least, it would appear that cycling is the new golf.

The venue for the launch was Ilkley Tennis & Squash Club, the approach was hindered by a substantial descent (which meant a subsequent climb). The plan was to have a short rapid ride with David before returning for a feast prepared by one of the cyclists, Alan Murchison, a Michelin star chef as well as a keen cyclist. In line with its ambition of enhancing the experience of the British cycling community, Maserati has recruited Alan, an age group duathlon World champion to apply his skills at one of the Tour de Yorkshire Ride feed stations. The final recipes will remain under wraps until the day but Alan will use fresh Yorkshire produce and apply an Italian twist to surprise and beguile riders, and hopefully give them the boost they need to see them home. The menu had been inspired by his ideas and his personal interpretation of the ideal foods required to sustain the average cyclist, before and after a lengthy ride, basically it was a mix of good carbs and quality locally sourced produce. Alan had prepared a taster session of his ideas for us to sample, each was accompanied with the cycling benefits of the ingredients. For starters we were exposed to Yorkshire asparagus, Parma ham, basil & fregola salad. Cycling benefits – fregola, originally produced in Sardinia, is rolled semolina roasted in the oven. It is very high in complex carbohydrates and is an amazing energy fuel. There is also smoked mackerel, rosemary, beetroot & potato salad. Cycling benefits – The mackerel provides fish oil & protein and the potato provides complex carbohydrates for energy. The beetroot is high in nitrates which aids transportation of oxygen to the blood. Two mains followed, rare breed Yorkshire lamb 'Shepherd's Pie' cooked with barolo. Cycling benefits – This dish provides protein from the lamb mince, complex carbohydrates from the potato and the red wine is an anti-oxidant, and Yorkshire pudding, red onion confit and spiced Italian sausage. Cycling benefits – The Yorkshire pudding provides complex carbohydrates and protein is provided by the sausage. Finally we moved onto desserts, Yorkshire rhubarb & ginger parkin 'tiramisu'. Cycling benefits – The ginger provides anti-flammatory benefits, rhubarb is high in nitrates and the milk will provide calcium and espresso & amaretti flapjacks. Cycling benefits – espresso for energy, oats for slow release energy and sugar for an instant lift.

After getting changed into my fetching Lycra attire I started to feel unwell, I admit I was feeling anxious about the ride but this was more than butterflies, I was bent double and resorted to throwing up in the spotless toilets. I had to accept begrudgingly that my brief ride was not going to happy, yet I was adamant that I would still interview David, I had two and a bit hours to recover.

I was feeling much better as the riders returned, plenty of fresh air and a constant flow of water worked. Whilst the rest of the journalists showered, a gap opened for me to chat to David earlier than expected. I have to admit I am no Jeremy Paxman, well I hope I am not but what followed was a really relaxed informal chat with the enigmatic Maserati ambassador.

David will be helping prepare participants for the Maserati Tour de Yorkshire Ride by offering expert insights into the particular challenges presented by the route's climbs and how best to prepare. The Scot, one of only two Britons to have worn the leader's jersey at all three Grands Tours, is a lifelong Maserati fan and lists the Maserati Ghibli II 2.8 GT as his dream car. He has never wavered in his dream to own a Ghibli, and despite previously coming close, is thrilled to finally take the keys to one as part of this new partnership.

Millar comments: "Just like the sport of cycling, motor sport is steeped in history, and the Maserati brand has played a key role in this rich heritage, through 100 years of engineering innovation. I am excited that two of my greatest passions in life are being combined and delighted to be involved from the start of what looks set to be a fantastic initiative."

Which is your favourite tour event?

What, like a stage race – the Tour de France, it's the one I fell in love with and it's the one event where my heart is, even though over the years its got bigger and bigger and crazier and crazier, it's still the only one that gives that magic feeling. I'm also a fan of the Vuelta (Tour of Spain) for different reasons.

Do you miss the cycling scene?

No, not really, that was one of the reasons why I chose to stop, because I wasn't enjoying it quite as much, it got to a point where it was time to move on. But I miss my friends and the camaraderie and the experiences, which I will never have again, how deep we were at times, which I will definitely miss. But I have to remember how much it hurt, it's easy to look through rose tinted glasses after a while, and wish I was still racing, and then you have to remember it was pretty much horrible most of the time.

How did you feel about missing the 2014 Tour de France?

I was gutted, I still am gutted. I think I will always be.

Do you think you could have produced?

I would have performed 100%. After 18 years, I know what I am capable of, but, hey, c'est la vie.

Any plans to set up your own cycling team?

No, F&&k that, it's a thankless job, the amount of effort you have to put in and, to be honest, I have had the best job in cycling, a racer. I just don't want to manage a team or be a team boss. I need to expand my horizons and do something different.

The recent CIRC report alleging that 90% of the Peloton are still doping, what's your thoughts?

I thought it was very irresponsible of the commission to put something like that, where it's one persons opinion, and for them to say it's from a respected pro but they are anonymous, so we need to be a judge if they are a respected pro or not. Besides, it is just not true; it's not based on any facts. Again, I feel it was very irresponsible, there are so many clean guys out there winning the biggest races, but then the headline across the World is the Peloton is still doping.

What do you like doing in your downtime?

Nothing, I'm really lazy... Actually, I like gardening now. At my new house in Girona, I am just planting a whole garden, checking my trees and wandering around the place.

Is your schedule as busy now in comparison to when you were cycling?

It has its moments, this week and next week are really busy. Hopefully the whole of April I will be at home. It's a lot better than it was, ten times better and that was another main reason why I stopped' I didn't want to travel as much.

Why choose Girona as home?

It's great for cycling, real community now. When we started, the community wasn't so big but, in the last seven or eight years, it has become massive; not that we are involved directly with it as we are located out of the town. It's just a great place to be a pro cyclist, the terrain, the roads, close proximity to airports. It's a no brainer really!

What is the best bike you have ridden?

I don't know, at that level they are all kind of good, especially as a pro. The bikes we use are obviously the latest models. Nowadays they are all so similar.

Are they made to measure?

My Cervelo was made to measure, it's the only Cervelo to have been made to measure and that was because I have a long back so I need to have a really long top tube. I had a 56cm seat tube and a 61cm top tube, I just don't fit on normal bikes but other than that, most of the time I was on standard bikes.

A great weekend, with great people in Clitheroe. (May 2015)

I arrived, fatigued, after crossing from the east coast and the mildly windswept coastline of Scarborough. (Tour de Yorkshire, but that's for another day).

I had just ventured over the border from the rose of Yorkshire to the rose of Lancashire, the perceived hatred is a publicity gimmick which does promote interest but in reality is nothing more than light-hearted banter.

As a cyclist, you get to visit some salient places, that most who travel at speed in metallic monsters fail to see or experience. Clitheroe was such a place, historic narrow streets and the trip advisor favourite, a castle! The venue for my inspired weekend was Waddow Hall, just on the outskirts of the town. I had been invited to speak at the inaugural Cycle Touring Festival (did they have any idea what they were letting themselves for?). My home for the weekend was under canvas and after a very much blundered erection (still on about the tent) I eventually had time to speak with my neighbour. This grey-haired adonis appeared from a simple canvas shell, I immediately recognised him as Stephen Lord (I think the name badge gave it away, I jest!). I immediately liked the guy, he was the epitome of amiable and considering he is 'Mr Adventure Cycling' there was not a pretentious bone in his ageing (LOL) body.

After all the introductions and explanations about itineraries etc, it was time for, normally I would say bed but 'Cold Tent' was more appropriate. I slept relatively 'Tent Like' – uncomfortable, cold, damp, but always memorable. The morning and some heat was overdue and as I was wiping the dribble from my face, Mr Adventure Cycling appeared, fresh faced and offering a homemade hot beverage.

That subsequent coffee sweetened with honey was absolutely charming, but so was the man himself. The expert barista awoke me the next morning with the same steaming infusion of coffee beans and honey, and it's something that I will never forget.

The Saturday for me personally was extremely chaotic, I had to talk early on about 'Writing for a Magazine'. The panel consisted of Ruth Jarvis and myself. The atmosphere was relaxed and the questions and interest flowed. I was amazed at how many people had attended, especially this early on a Saturday morning, the undeniable draw was Ruth, who is one nice lady with a plethora of information and advice which she has acquired throughout her illustrious career.

I personally find people are always positive and keen to write but getting them to actually produce, is so difficult. The main barrier is the fact that they are worried that their words won't be good enough, and I understand nobody likes rejection, but I invariably find that the majority of the submissions I receive are of a high standard and ultimately my job, as editor, is to fit their words to meet the expectations of our readership. In saying that, I tend to not change people's words too much, otherwise they will eventually become my words, which is inherently wrong, and ultimately detracts from the vision of the writer. The hour long session whizzed by, questions were relentless and I was glad that so many people were interested.

Next up was UK and Ireland, in the BIG room. On the panel was myself and the lovely Anna Hughes, who is a cycling guide, but is most famous for her book 'Eat, Sleep, Cycle'. The room was full, an eager crowd awaiting our words.

Thankfully we both held their concentration, I waffled about Ireland, especially Connemara and specifically the 'Wild Atlantic Way' and she explained in detail her trek around the coast of Britian

Then after lunch, it was Europe with Kev Shannon and Hannah Reynolds. Kev has spent a lot of time cycling in Serbia – part of the old Yugoslavia – and Turkey, and Hannah as well as being a fitness editor for Cycling Active, is also a minefield of information on France. I love her book, 'France en Vélo', written with John Walsh, the illustrations are sensational, the feel just promotes a raw gallicness (I don't care if it's not a word, it portrays how exceptional it is).

Everybody mixed happily that evening. Part of it was pre-occupied with me typing up some words and then Kev, Anna and I, and the idea of Paul Cheese, who I had featured in an article about his exploits following town names with a connection to cheese throughout Europe. We simply acted like children, hilarity, giggles, cheese related joviality, I will not forget the fun.

I had agreed to mark a Writing Competition, aided by Anna and Kev. In total, we received fifteen entries and all were special in their own way. The criterion was to write a simple three hundred words on any subject, patently bike related. The standard was amazing and, in the end, I decided that Jo Gibson was a worthy winner; her first-class, evocative detail of her trip around Thailand was just ace. Well done to everyone who took part!

This group of like-minded, beautiful (I mean you, Kev) and sociable people, have already been approached to pen some words for me, selfishly it's not about the writing, it's about their personalities, after just a couple of days in their company I feel attached to some bizarre pedalling fraternity. Cyclists are weird, I know because my DNA is overwhelmed by all things two wheeled, I admit it (crikey I feel like I am in rehab) we invariably are selfish, committed, resolute but ultimately likeable human beings. There is no pretension, this small group of speakers are well –known authors, successful in their own way but what a great bunch and hopefully they will become great friends and not just the stereotypical acquaintances. Personally I would bloody miss the banter and interactions that ultimately Laura and Tim nurtured by accident, the success of the festival will have even surprised them, it will clearly be an annual addition to my calendar. Canada, Taiwan, China, are great (and I am a lucky chap to visit these places) but in reality Clitheroe in the rain with Stephen Lord's sublime coffee beats them all! Great people, great atmosphere, great kebabs (don't ask), just simply great fun. Roll on next year! (To be honest, I might not get invited back!)

dublinbikes, what an astonishing success (April 2015)

Everybody is raving about the new scheme, dublinbikes. The city is the ideal choice to pedal on a bike; the centre is unfortunately renowned for its congestion, so anything that can ease the impact and improve the environment has to be applauded. The scheme has been in operation since 2009 and is sponsored by JCDecaux. It was the seventeenth city to implement such an initiative and, in June 2014, it was announced that Coca-Cola Zero would become a commercial partner for three years.

The Coca-Cola Zero brand is immediately recognisable, blazoned across each individual bike, the scheme simply offers a self-service bike rental system (similar to the schemes seen across the world, especially London) and is open to everyone from fourteen years of age. It's an easy, stress-free and convenient way to negotiate the city whether commuting or just to see the sights.

The system has proved to be an amazing success, it was reported that in the first ten months there were over 37,000 users, over 828, 000 journeys with remarkably no accidents, no vandalism and only one theft.

It's relatively cheap to use the system, with the dublinbikes scheme you have to initially subscribe, this is not as onerous or pricey as it sounds, and it gives the subscriber access to unlimited rentals. An annual subscription costs €20 or a short-term three day ticket is €5. As with most of these schemes, the first half hour of every journey is free, and then after, certain charges apply: one hour is €0.50, two hours €1.50, three hours €3.50 and four hours €6.50. From four hours onwards, each extra thirty minutes incurs a charge of €2, but through research it is acknowledged that the majority of journeys (95%) last less than thirty minutes, making them free of any charges.

The bicycle stock is as expected, robust and substantially weighty but not at detriment to the ride; they come with three gears which change (smoothly) utilising the Shimano Nexus twist and grip shifters. With all these types of bikes there is LED lighting at the front and rear, powered by a hub dynamo with a meaty looking integrated locking system and kick stand.

All the stations are equipped for 'Annual or 3 Day Ticket Users' with a number of terminals being 'Credit Card enabled' allowing you to purchase a 3 Day Ticket direct. Once purchased, you can use this card in a similar fashion. There are currently forty-seven stations across the city, and all are open between the hours of 05:00a.m. and 00:30a.m., but this is constantly growing as demand increases.

Hiring a bike.

The scheme is very easy to use; there are instructions on each individual terminal menu on how to rent and return the bikes. You can also view the availability of bikes and stands by downloading the Coca-Cola Zero dublinbikes App, which is suitable for all android and other smartphones. To hire, simply log in at any terminal using your Annual Card or 3 Day Ticket. Enter your PIN and select an available bike on screen, you then have sixty seconds to press the unlocking button on the specific stand of the bike you have chosen. Once you have pressed the button you have five seconds to remove bike from the stand.

Returning a Bike.

Simply locate the nearest station with available stands. An audio signal of two 'beeps' and a green indicator light on the stand confirm that the bike is locked correctly. If there are no available stands in your vicinity, then you will need to use the terminal to find the next nearest station with spaces. You are given an extra fifteen minutes free of charge to get to this new location. It's essential that you check the bike is locked correctly, otherwise you will be liable if the bike goes missing.

Exploration.

The city is absorbed by the dublinbikes scheme; young, old, athletic and not so athletic happily navigate the busy streets occupied with an endless array of cars, buses and trams. Access to the sights and places of interest is simple via bike: Trinity College (the home of the Book of Kells), Dublin Castle, The National Museum of Ireland and the Temple Bar area. The city is an attractive mix of nostalgia and modernity, historic events have unequivocally created a resolute determination which is demonstrated in the classic and charming architecture. Initially I made my way along Pearce Street, in search of the Library, I always venture to a local library to research up on interesting facts. The area was overflowing with students, emphasising the city's academic standing, the library was only a short pedal away. Unfortunately it was closed, so I pedalled back towards the city centre. We are all aware of the legendary Irish hospitality and I can assure you that it is completely true, their infectious positivity and all-round party/laidback approach to life should be experienced once in any human's life (like a pilgrimage of frivolity).

Pearce Street leads onto the commercial heartbeat of the city and the beautiful Trinity College. Everywhere roads are eclipsed by buses, trams and a conveyor belt of cyclists. The amount of people utilising dublinbikes was astonishing, every other bike was blazoned in the Coca-Cola Zero emblem, there were plenty of empty stations as I made my way around the city, which was great and demonstrates how committed the locals are to cycling but should be recognised as a reason to increase/extend the amount of stations to accommodate demand. It's that old historical problem of practicability, how much money do you invest and what is the ultimate yield (not sure what that means but it sounds good), following my limited immersion, it's self-evident the demand is currently out-weighing the availability. I was pleased to discover that dublinbikes are extending the product to meet some of the gaps. The concept is an ideal match for the city, which will unquestionably increase and, most importantly, get young and old, locals or visitors out and about on a bicycle. Trust me, there is loads to see!

Who is Mick Ives?
(February 2015)

On a mediocre day in the Capital at the London Bike Show, I had a chance meeting with a somewhat ageing (he won't mind that description) lean fit looking gentleman. This guy just oozed enthusiasm and his passion for cycling was overwhelming. We chatted for a while and, before he departed, I agreed to attend a launch event for his cycling team in the Midlands, Coventry to be precise.

Mick Ives at 75 has had an illustrious career on two wheels being a professional cyclist for many years and the plaudits are endless and impressive. He has been UCI World Masters Cycling Champion five times, British National Cycling Champion sixty-two times (which is completely astonishing) and at one time he was the manager of the Great British Cycling Team and the National Coach. But overall he is just a bloody nice likeable passionate chap.

He now runs the very successful Team Jewson MI Racing which he formed in 1997 and during that period they have won over one thousand races throughout the UK and mainland Europe. The strangest fact I discovered about this comparatively crazy pensioner was that he completed the Tour de France in 2005, riding alone two days ahead of the big race which, for anyone, is an amazing feat, but for a pensioner is absolutely extraordinary.

I arrived at a stereotypical non-descript industrial estate on the outskirts of the city early on a bright Saturday morning. Bikes adorned tops of cars, vans blazoned with sponsors names, gazebo's glistening in the sunshine, this was clearly serious stuff.

There was plenty of time before the team were introduced so I mingled and immersed myself in the well-stocked smorgasbord of healthy delights on offer. After stuffing my pockets with apples and bananas (ok, and the odd digestive!), it was finally time to meet the eclectic team.

The team rides across various disciplines (Road racing, Track, Time Trials, Triathlons, Mountain Biking, Tandem Races, Hill Climbs and Cyclo-Cross) and various age ranges (the youngest are just teenagers and the oldest are in their seventies) but don't compete in the more specialised BMX arena. As they were all introduced individually by Mick, it was obvious that he was proud, like a father, of each and every one. The team's main sponsor is Jewson and their logo sits prominently on their colourful and dynamic team jerseys.

The presentation was informal but well delivered and each rider's individual achievements were detailed by their inspirational leader. It was great to see a real camaraderie as they approached the makeshift stage. What was admirable, and ultimately inspiring, was the unexpected body shapes, some with remarkably rotund physiques, more akin to the less athletic among us. Even more noticeable was the firm thighs and prominent veins you would expect from the Lance Armstrong types (the disgraced American is maybe not the best example but it demonstrates the fitness of these Lycra clad individuals). It was safe to say this group of pedallers were seriously fit and dedicated to all things cycling. What followed was an endless cavalcade of photos and cups of coffee. Helmets on, helmets off, shoes on, shoes off, sugar, no sugar, you get the picture. Thankfully, I eventually did, and my camera was brimming with some stylish arty images of these dedicated athletes. As the crowds dwindled and the Lycra was replaced by the casuals of Joe Public, I recognised that this group of cyclists were just average human beings but with one collective goal, to be the best they can regardless of age, gender or background. The infectious resilience and commitment of Mick has rubbed off on this cycling family and I don my hat to this nirvana of pedalling, please can I join, but not yet as I am far too busy!

I will certainly be keeping MI Racing on my and Cadence Cycling's radar, the group is a credit to their youthful leader. He will be going on long after I have hung up my helmet, I'm sure of it

La Vélo Francette – a bike, the rivers and sublime isolation (June 2015)

The Mayenne, once again I would have to google its location, which is a common occurrence nowadays, not only to me but to the British nation. I find the whole ignorance of the French departments and regions an embarrassment. My initial destination was Laval, to be honest I had never heard of the place (adhering to the stereotype), however my journeys end was to be Angers which I was familiar with (hooray!) following an exhausting but rewarding visit in June last year to cover the Anjou Vélo Vintage. I had read that Laval also has a similar event the Vélo Agglo Rétro, which I had just missed, usually held mid-June.

As usual my expectations were high and this area (in and around the Loire Valley) never fails to impress, with a mix of glorious surroundings dotted with picturesque villages and countless châteaus, together with a simple isolation.

The plan was to discover La Vélo Francette which trails its way south from the English Channel at Ouistreham and finally empties into the Atlantic near La Rochelle.

The Mayenne is one of the smallest departments in France and is situated in the west, south of Normandy, close to Brittany and the Loire Valley. That's the geography lesson over! The region is easily accessible from the UK, the ferry port of Ouistreham is only a couple of hours by car, there are flights from London City Airport to Angers and the train (my preferred choice) from London St Pancras to Gare-du-Nord with Eurostar, then Montparnasse to Laval, but you can also go directly to Angers with SNCF. The booking process is simple, Rail Europe will happily sort your itinerary so that you have realistic window to get across Paris to make your connection, it's a great experience which I always revel in.

Day One – jeudi.

I didn't sleep too well. It wasn't the bed, the room or the heat; I just couldn't switch off my mind. Breakfast consisted of a mountain of pancakes and fruit, healthy and nutritious. I unfortunately hadn't time to see much of Laval, with my late arrival and usual early start, time was limited. However, what I did see was a collection of beautiful, simple buildings and narrow labyrinthine streets and alleys. Its heart is the wonderful Mayenne river and the spectacular elevated château, imposingly standing guard over the town. No matter how hard I tried I wouldn't get lost, La Vélo Francette follows the sluggish Mayenne river all the way to Angers, where it meets the Maine river. This morning the château was basking in the sunlight, its eleventh century structure proudly dominating from its strategic position. The route south was originally used for horses to tow barges, but nowadays is comfortable with more refined leisure activities, cycling, walking and jogging. Its official title is 'le Chemin de halage' and offers the traveller an overwhelming tranquillity. It has now become a conservation area and the track consists predominately of gravel, with limited or no tarmac, the surroundings a glut of flat agricultural farmland, with the occasional foray into luscious tree cover. Initially the route was busy with other cyclists, ramblers and the occasional interloper foraging for wild fruit on the riverbank. Every enjoyable kilometre is beautifully signed, so, in reality, there is no need for a map; orientation is simple. A perfect description is 'Slow Tourism' The dusty gravel tracks reward the cyclists with breathtaking views of the unspoilt countryside.

As I pedalled, it wasn't difficult to imagine the boat men, whose 'garbes' (merchandise boats), up to thirty metres long, were dragged along by the horses. The constant hustle of commerce is long gone but thankfully their legacy is still very evident. There were plenty of châteaus dotted along this section; however the majority were privately owned and not open to the public, which was a shame.

I stopped for a coffee in idyllic surroundings beside the lock at La Benâtre, the setting was magical with a lock and mill my only company. The coffee was cheap, the service more than friendly, a great place in exquisite soothing environs. The sun was happily radiating a substantial heat, my water consumption was intense. As I continued, the solitude was infectious; the shaded area reassuringly frequent, I encountered several other cyclists, all with beaming smiles, all exchanged friendly 'Bonjour'

The Vélo Francette, is just one of many cycle routes dissecting France. The route travels 630 km from Ouistreham in the north and La Manche (English Channel), meandering south towards the Atlantic and La Rochelle; it allows the rider to discover seven departments, three regional natural parks and plenty of character filled villages and towns. The route is a mix of isolated country lanes, gravel tracks and green routes. Along the route there is an extensive network of businesses and services equipped to welcome the bike, these are identified by the 'Accueil Vélo' label and are conveniently located less than five km from the trail. The route connects the Véloscénie in the north with La Loire a Vélo, south of Angers.

The river is home to a wide diversity of fish, grass snakes (eekk) and plenty of frogs. Its riverbanks are popular with local fishermen attempting to land that big catch; the most common species are carp, roach, zander and pike. Its enclosed valley creates an enchanting location to pedal, limited wind and attractive winding contours add to sensation of solitude. The steep sides have allowed for continual isolation as construction is prohibited along its banks, with villages situated a short distance from the water along ancient roads which run parallel to the river. The river gives the gentle rolling landscape of pasture and swaying fields, its sublime character.

I halted once again, the temperature required so, the area is dominated by the river. There are plenty of outlets to hire boats and explore from the water.

Château-Gontier is a lovely place; it is classed as one of the most beautiful small villages in France with a collection of medieval façades, winding narrow streets and a clean welcoming ambience. I paused for a coffee in the main square opposite the beautiful Hôtel de Ville, it provided me with the tantalising prospect of spying, but I like to think of it as learning about the culture and the local community (it's less likely to get me locked up!) My overnight stop was at the ostentatious Parc and Spa hotel which is conveniently located a short distance from the centre. It's a stunning place; you can smell the history as you enter via reception. The building was constructed in the nineteenth Century and sits amongst some beautifully manicured lawns. Modernity is satisfied by WiFi and a spa area, offering a heated swimming pool, sauna, jacuzzi. Its slightly elevated position blocks out the rather busy road below and provides some stunning views back towards the centre.

My bike was arranged by Mayenne Tourisme which they obtained from Vert-event Angers. The price of rental is calculated by the amount of days you have the bike, included is a helmet, anti-theft device, pump and repair kit. You can also arrange for the bike to be delivered to your place of residence. Extra options include luggage transfer, children's trailers and baby seats. So there is no reason for anybody to be omitted from a ride.

Day Two – vendredi.

After a lovely peaceful breakfast, I departed Château-Gontier with some sadness. I reacquainted myself with the Mayenne and headed south. The route would eventually see me entering a different department, the Maine-et-Loire or Anjou region. I was feeling rather lethargic this morning, my physical condition was relatively ok, but my legs just couldn't be bothered with this whole pedalling thing, they had decided to go on strike! I reassured myself that this unusual malaise would pass as the day progressed. Again the weather was stifling, the air was limited, the heat incessant. The river appeared more relaxed than yesterday, its pace snail like, the only speedy interlopers were the odd leisure cruiser. On several occasions, I encountered a convoy of school children exploring the riverbank by bike; as I passed, the echoes of 'Attention au vélo' pierced the otherwise tranquil surroundings.

In no time I had breezed past the sign for Daon, my legs had finally decided to wake from their slumber and my progress was good, my water intake was as expected frequent.

I passed several well-presented campsites; all appeared busy with plenty of people enjoying the water by canoe.

I had opted for a slight detour to Le Lion d'Angers, mainly in search of lunch but the name did intrigue. For the first time I left the banks of the Mayenne and followed the Oudon river into the town. The centre was full of children of all ages and I was surprised to discover, in the country renowned for its gastronomy, their preferred option for lunch appeared to be the kebab, of the Turkish variety. I applied the 'When in Rome' ideology and followed suit. I found some shade on the banks of the Oudon and ate.

The section of La Vélo Francette south of the town is still under development so I had to travel over a bridge and follow the river on the opposite side for several kilometres before crossing the river once again. The local children use its elevated position to dive into the watery chasm below, the simple joys of childhood.

I was once again following the Mayenne, unfortunately my determination and blinkered concentration resulted in me completely bypassing Grez-Neuville. The trail deteriorated significantly, the surface a mix of boulders, pot holes and all kinds of debris. After checking with a group of locals swimming in the waters, I headed back towards a crêperie and Grez-Neuville.

The village was separated by the river, the right side was previous referred to as Neuville and the left Grez, but after the construction of the bridge, they amalgamated to be known as Grez-Neuville. My accommodation was in the Grez part and was described in the itinerary as a B&B.

Côté Rivère; wow, wow, wow, an oasis of unimaginable delights. This was introduced by the owners Sandrine and Benoit as a B&B, but please remove any preconceptions of the typical B&B you find back home (you know, run by Freda and over-run with paisley) , this place was magnificent. Directly on the riverbank, its elevated position provided a stunning panorama of the river. I was given the newly furbished extension which was a stunning, modern and minimalistic self-contained annexe just off the main lounge area. It had a plethora of mod-cons, WiFi, TV, an electric bed (similar to the ones in hospital) its main purpose is to allow for uninterrupted views of the river whilst in repose, and a snazzy one touch device which operates the lights remotely (I briefly felt like Gadget Man). An exquisite welcome message was scrawled on a simple blackboard. The décor was sublime, a mix of traditional exposed stonework and a splash of vibrant colours, lifting the room. The owners were obviously proud of their property and it showed; they have sourced the most coveted items, meticulously utilising an array of understated French accessories, and the result is a warming and modern rural retreat. Through the French doors was a quaint welcoming veranda, with views of the inviting pool and beautifully manicured garden. What more can I say, the place was a magical haven. To describe it as a B&B, was a complete underestimation of its qualities, the owners have created utopia in rural France, C'est très très bien, Sandrine et Benoit.

That evening I was lucky enough to eat with family, the barbecue was fired up, the food was superb and so was the company, the conversation and laughter flowed. As the sun retired the river took on a completely different character, with limited light pollution the sky was dazzling and the nocturnal wildlife came alive, bats happily infiltrated the surroundings. I was treated to my own personal lullaby as the distance sound of the music festival in nearby Le Lion d'Angers soothed me to sleep

Day Three – samedi.

Why not? It would be rude not to take a plunge in the pool. I was trying to convince myself as I awoke; the sun was already streaming through the blinds. It was going to be another hot day in the saddle, Angers was my focus. However I had breakfast to negotiate, followed by an invigorating cold plunge, what a great start to any day. Life has its hardships but occasionally you experience a brief moment in time when life is wondrous, that moment was now the only thing missing was the presence of my wife, then I would be living the dream, the French dream.

Benoit offered to accompany me the eight kilometres to Feneu and my meeting point with Nathalie. We followed the roadway, it was deserted which allowed us to continue our lively conversation from the previous evening.

Nathalie arrived on time, I said farewell to Benoit and we pedalled off towards Angers. Nathalie explained she works for Anjou Tourisme, and obviously cycles a lot, considering her rather athletic disposition. We followed the Mayenne at a relaxing pace which was good, the surroundings a mirror image of the previous two days. We breezed past Montreuil-Juigné, stopping by the ferry for Île St-Aubin, Nathalie explained in detail the history of the area. Île St-Aubin is located on a vast wetland, it is only accessible in the summer months, as it is completely immersed in water at other times. It offers a wonderfully diverse environment and ecosystem, home to extraordinary amounts of plant and animal life.

A short pedal ride away was Terra Botanica. Europe's first themed park for plant life and nature (it doesn't sound that interesting, especially for the less green fingered like me, but it was and you could be surprised). It offers over forty differing interactive attractions and plays on your senses, the aromas and seductive tranquillity are overwhelming. The highlight is a trip on the recently installed ballon. The tethered attraction allows thirty passengers to soar above the park to the dizzy heights of 150m, the panorama of the city and river basin are tremendous, definitely not to be missed. Nathalie said farewell, allowing me to explore at my own pace.

After several enjoyable hours, I pedalled off towards Angers and Le Grand Hôtel de la Gare, which would be my base for the next two nights.

Day Four – dimanche.

Everywhere I went, people were telling me I had to pedal to Bouchemaine and La Pointe. The area is special due to the fact that it is at the confluence of La Maine and La Loire rivers. Over breakfast, I pondered 'La Loire à Vélo' map; the route was obviously popular and would transport me along the Loire easterly, before heading north at La Daguenière through the slate mines and back into Angers.

However, before my ride I had to meet with a local guide who would show me the delights of the city. Surprisingly she was English, Liz has been a resident of the area for twenty years and I immediately liked her. Her sense of humour and all round disposition were infectious. We had a relatively small window to explore so off we went, the city was so quiet, the locals still in bed recovering from the night before. As we walked, Liz created images of the past in her animated simple words. I was grateful that she didn't bombard me with a cavalcade of historical facts, her great skill was to assess each individual and cater the conversation to fit their needs. The city is full of history, the site has been occupied for thousands of years and was a prominent Roman settlement. Unfortunately, a large amount of buildings suffered devastation at the hands of the allies, but thankfully the Château and Cathédrale remained unscathed. The château is emblematic of the city, it's undoubtedly a stunning structure and the promontory has been the location of fortification since IXth Century (but the present building dates back from the XIIIth Century) Throughout history the building was expanded and grew to its current stature, the highlight and world famous attraction is the Tapestry of the Apocalypse, the World's largest known medieval tapestry . Housed in modern surroundings, in complete contrast to the hand-stitched beauty on display, it evokes a slightly emotional reaction. The area is partially lit to protect its colours which are more pastel, the vibrancy long gone. It's a dramatic adaption of good versus evil, beautifully presented and has to be seen in person. Nowadays with technology and endless access to literature, some feel the remote experience is sufficient, I disagree, to be able to completely immerse, interact and treat your senses cannot be underestimated, especially with this exceptional work of art, so put down your iPad and get out and explore.

From the château, we briefly visited La Cathédrale Saint Maurice, the clarity of the light enhancing its beauty. Its interior is stunning, the only light provided by the ornate, colourful Renaissance stained glass windows. A service was due to take place so we departed. At the rear of the building is La Place Sainte Croix, the ancient heart of the city, lined with a lovely array of historic buildings including the sixteenth Century Maison d'Adam, a merchants house, believed to be the oldest in the city, with its lower floor housing a contemporary boutique style shop. The upper floors contain an exquisite collection of wonderfully ornate narrative carvings set amongst its splendid timber frame. They bring the building to life, Liz pointed out the cheeky figure of a man who appears to possess three testicles, a point of hilarity amongst the locals.

Next up was the Musée des Beaux Arts (in the cultural district), this modern building provides an extensive history of the city, through differing medias. It was great to be able to attribute Liz's words to certain exhibits. After a coffee in the wide esplanade of La Place du Railliement, we headed back to the hotel, the La Loire à Vélo was beckoning. The last three hours had flown by, I knew more about the city than I ever thought possible, when and (not if) you visit the city my best piece of advice is contact the Office de Tourisme a.s.a.p and arrange sometime with a guide, you won't regret it and it beats self-orientation. Merci Liz pour votre aide pour mon illumination culturelle.

As I left the city I spied the temperature, an unwelcoming 34°C was on display, and my hope was for some shade as I explored the La Loire à Vélo. Almost immediately the urban surroundings were replaced by greenery. The La Loire à Vélo hugs the river in a similar vein to the Mayenne and La Vélo Francette. It's impossible to get lost. It's a haven for hikers, walkers and cyclists with a wealth of tidy, well-signed trails. The route was busy with cyclists of all ages but never impacted on the overall enjoyment. The surface is well maintained, my direction east following the signs for Saumur was unhindered, I halted briefly by the Lac de Maine in the protection of verdant foliage. I breezed through Bouchemaine and dissected a park brimming with families enjoying picnic's in the shade of the trees. My arrival in La Pointe was greeted by a mass of people, the village was hosting an arts festival, open houses selling all manner of creative products and a lone musician entertaining the crowds the accompanying tagline 'A journey of art through the gardens of La Pointe' so appropriate. The whole area exuded a colourful, friendly and understated ambivalence. I sat for a while and listened to the typically French Répertoire from the soloist, the experience mesmerising enhanced by the waters providing a dramatic backdrop.

I retraced my way back towards Bouchemaine and the signed route east, the heat was incessant, so in the small domain of Port Thibault I detoured towards the water, this section of river offers a welcoming collection of beach-like areas, the location popular with sun-worshippers and families cooling off, children playing noisily, it was a great spot. After arduously dragging my transportation across the sand, a much needed dip in the inviting water was a definite. Standing ankle deep initially, I discovered the water was rather welcoming so, stripping down to my boxers (not a great image), I tentatively entered the river. It was surprisingly warm and full immersion quickly followed.

Following my impromptu dip I dragged my bike back to civilisation and continued my adventure eastwards. The trail was deserted; my only company was the noisy local bird community. The Loire was France's biggest shipping channel from the fifteenth to the nineteenth Century, transporting all types of goods up and down the river with the fûtreaux and other smaller boats ploughing up and down, until the railway sounded their death knell from 1850 to the beginning of the twentieth century, nowadays the commerce has declined replaced by fûtreaux, toues and plates – traditional boats happily accommodating the influx of tourists and fisherman who came to enjoy the exceptional ecosystem on its banks. There is no denying the river still plays an important part of community life. In La Daguenièrie I stopped to rehydrate and then left La Loire heading north towards the slate mines and Angers. There is something romantic about La Loire, it's hard to identify or explain but it evokes an inner peace and contentment. The rigours of modernity banished, only simple nature and exploration remain; it's a wonderful phenomenon and should be experienced by everyone, regardless of age or physical condition.

The 'Blue Gold' of Angers is renowned worldwide for its quality, it was extracted in the slate quarries 'officially' as early as the fifteenth Century, but probably exploited since Neolithic times in and around Trélazé, however, most recently there has been a significant decline in production but Ardoise slate has left a legacy on the city, adorning many fine buildings. I was exposed to the colourful palette of its history as I pedalled back towards the city centre and the confines of La Place de Railliement, and a coffee.

La Vélo Francette is not just a cycle trail, it's a stunning portal into rural France, I have pedalled many of these exceptional routes throughout France but the isolation I encountered between Laval and Angers was astonishing. The mystical stillness was overwhelming, the river laid-back as it reluctantly meets the Maine in Angers. The river is the life blood of the area and conceals some beautiful, relatively untouched villages and towns. The jewel amongst many jewels was La Pointe-Bouchemaine, it was a slightly energetic place when I visited, but I can imagine when the festivals are long gone, it becomes a glorious sleepy domain that feels like it is at the end of the world as the La Loire and Maine rivers converge. You will be hard pressed to find a better, more loved cycle route across France and even Europe, that's how much I enjoyed my short but hypnotic journey.

Is China really a great place to cycle? (April 2015)

The bike is a great method of getting about in China's cities and also an agreeable alternative to the car when exploring the countryside, as well as being an authentic way of see the real China. Unfortunately due to the considerable size of the country you will have to combine your cycling with much quicker methods of transport, i.e, trains, boats, planes, if you want to explore further into the provinces. The next few pages will hopefully give you a brief insight into cycling in China, I visit some of the best known cities and sights as well as venturing off the beaten track to discover the real China.

Our first destination was Shanghai, the new shiny face of China. The city is still in its adolescence but is home to approximately 25 million people (and growing!). It's truly a city where east meets west, colourful, chaotic and full of contradictions. The city has plenty of history but it's overshadowed by the metallic giants of globalisation and business. The majority of the locals utilise the buses and the subway, the roads are relatively quiet due to the requirement to pay millions of Yuan for a Shanghai number plate. This costly process significantly reduces the amount of locals who can afford the luxury of a car, which was the reason for the authorities imposing the legislation in the first place. The city is an exception to other Chinese cities: the bike is rarely used or seen. Don't get me wrong, the bike is still present but clearly not as popular and the majority of riders don face masks in an attempt to reduce the risk from pollution. The city is ruled by the underground, which is relatively cheap, making it an obvious choice with the locals and visitors alike. The efficiency and ease of the public transport deters people from venturing out on the bike, which is a surprise considering the reduction in the volume of cars and the standard (lack of) of driving, in comparison to other Chinese cities. The only exception is the bewitching French Concession district, the pleasant tree-lined avenues are awash with the bike. The area retains a simple but elegant character, unmistakably western in influence, it's home to a mass of independent retailers, cafés and restaurants. Once the home of the city's explorer types and writers, it maintains an artistic inspirational flair. The lack of bikes is a real shame because the city, especially the Bund, is a great setting to pedal and at night the lights set a dramatic backdrop, the views are mesmerising as you gaze over the Huangpu river towards the Pudong skyline, and, if you turn your eyes in the other direction, the view of the Puxi skyline, with its art-deco and gothic architecture, is a match for the globes of steel and endless glass. This perfectly highlights the rapid growth that will no doubt make China the World's number one super power that it aspires to, if isn't already!

Bike hire outlets can be found in most tourist locations, with the majority of youth hostels offering bicycles for rental. Normal bikes can be hired by the day or by the hour, and rental prices vary depending on the location, but you can pay as little as ¥10 or ¥15 per day in big cities, like Beijing. Most outlets will ask for a substantial deposit of around ¥500.

Beijing is an enigma. It's one of my favourite cities; I am both intrigued and dismayed by the fact that poverty is acceptable and sits bizarrely comfortable with the money and luxury of the mega rich. The Hutongs are outshone by the humble bike, with brightly decorated rickshaws around every corner. I understand that they are all part of the tourist trade, providing visitors with a stereotypical view of China, and Beijing. Cynically it does mean that the real China is overshadowed by the romantic image that they evoke but for the locals I recognise it's a method of generating a moderately good income, in-comparison to most of the populace. At any rate, it was evident there were less bicycles on the roads since my last visit. Was this due to the typically British weather or more about choice being available for the residents, especially with important issues like convenience and safety? Or, controversially, is it down to the levels of pollution? We had previously visited in 2012 and, on that occasion, the smog didn't appear to be as noticeable, or impact on our health or potential to see the sights.

Today pollution is an ever present contentious issue, especially in the larger cities, like Beijing and Guangzhou. The smog hangs over these cities almost daily. In 2012, when I was in the capital, I had read that the air quality index reading had been analysed and recorded at 2.5 micrometers, which, in normal-person-speak, means it can get into the blood stream and do damage to the respiratory system, and, on really bad days, the level can officially be classed as 'hazardous'. Many locals would argue that the levels are not too high, it is believed on average, an adult in Beijing inhales the equivalent of just one sixth of a cigarette a day which doesn't seem a lot. Nonetheless, you will still see plenty of cyclists donning reasonably attractive face masks, so the concerns and dangers are recognised and preventative measures are deemed a necessity by some. A recent report I read in China Daily (Thursday April 2nd 2015) stated 'Vehicles, coal burning, airborne dust and industrial production account for 85% to 90% of the major air pollution sources in most Chinese cities, with vehicles unapologetically being the biggest polluters in Beijing, Zhejiang, Guangzhou and Shenzhen.

Beijing city's new Air Quality Contingency Plan recently released a new pollution red alert with a lowered threshold, these alerts have been simplified in this new plan. They will be issued after the city's pollution Level Five reaches between two hundred and one, and three hundred on the Air Quality Index (AQI) for a certain number of days. A blue alert will be issued if it's predicted that Level Five pollution will descend on the capital for one day, a yellow alert will be issued if two days is likely and so a red alert, which was previously used when there were three consecutive days of Level Six pollution with an AQI reading over three hundred, will now be used when a Level Five pollution situation is predicted to continue for more than three days. The authorities recognise there is a growing issue around the City's air quality, which is why they are planning to ban vehicles with even and odd numbered licence plates from the roads on alternate days (when it issues a pollution red alert). Also, 30% of cars owned by government agencies will also be banished from the same roads, and some factories and corporations will also be required to limit or suspend production, as part of the new emergency measures. This can only be a positive step in addressing the issue of air quality especially for the exposed cyclists. Personally I would be interested to see the true figures on cycling for a pastime as opposed to cycling as an essential form of transportation (if only 1% of the populace pedalled for fun, that would equate to over thirteen million, at times it's difficult to contemplate the country's vast size). The Lycra market must be flagging (likely to be be dead in the water, I reckon); I was in Beijing for two days and I saw only a handful of cyclists wearing the stuff. The majority pedal as part of their daily lifestyle but even then the quantity on the roads appeared to have depleted since my last visit. I still find it astonishing and hilarious how they are happy to overload their bikes with all manner of things, tables, chairs, indeed any form of furniture (big or small) seem to be the most popular, yet anything goes!

Next up was Xian, one thousand kilometres inland and west of the capital. A great place to cycle and very popular with tourists are the magnificent City Walls. Most people associate Xian with the captivating Terracotta Warriors but the highlight for any keen cyclist is pedalling along the 13.7 kilometres of the ancient wall. Many visitors initially feel let down by the modern metropolis considering its magnificent legendary status and legacy. It was at the heart and terminus of the Silk Road and had a diversity of ethnic minorities unmatchable in China. Its glory days are over, still plenty of this rich heritage is still present, if you are prepared to venture out and explore. There are plenty of places to hire bicycles on the wall and the price is extremely cheap in comparison to western prices. ¥45 (approximately £4.50) gets you a reasonably robust bike, the wall's surface is bumpy but the views are well worth a sore derrière. Intricate and vibrantly coloured roof tiles, gilded cornices and the simple naivety of the lifestyle, steeped in history, and basic pleasures are on offer. Even so, on this trip the weather was behaving so typically British, cold, windy and wet, just like a summer back home. So we missed the wall initially in favour of the Big Goose Pagoda (and got bloody soaked!)

Alleluia, the next day brought fairer weather; even a ray of sun was visible, but only just. So we ventured tentatively towards the impressive ancient City Wall, which is not only the most complete city wall that has survived in China, it is also one of the largest and most complete ancient military defence system in the World. This was my second visit to this magnificent fortification which was built during the reign of Hongwu, the first Emperor of the Ming Dynasty. On that occasion the rain was incessant, the experience not too enjoyable but still undeniably memorable. Today the weather was markedly better so myself, my ever patient wife and two of my five children agreed to hire two tandems and pedal along a part of the wall, I assured them the experience would be unforgettable. So with the adults in front and the kids holding up the rear (ideally placed for the occasional bout of flatulence) we set off from the East Gate. The surface is in relatively good condition, considering its age, with the odd missing section or uneven stones but the bikes adequate suspension coped with any deviations, protecting the exposed buttocks. The wall affords some gripping views, the inner section is influenced by traditional buildings and the outer a mass of high rise modernity, shimmering in the sunlight. There were plenty of others experiencing the wall by bike and there was no lack of places to hire. Although, if you are feeling truly lazy you can be whisked around in a golf cart which is significantly more expensive and less rewarding. As we made good progress, the unimaginable became a reality, could we cycle the whole 13.7 kilometres in the allotted time (just over an hour). Why not? If we worked together, it was a definite possibility. So, with an increased determination, we pushed on, our legs resembling the precision of pistons in full flow. Back in time, the wall originally enclosed eighty-three square kilometres, an area in fact seven times larger than the city centre. Now that would have been a step too far!

We stopped occasionally in the shadows of several ornate look out towers, the resonant decoration so mesmerising. The weather was still behaving, the city is one of my personal favourite Chinese cities to cycle, there are so my magnificent historical sights in close proximity: the City Walls, The Big Goose Pagoda, The Little Goose Pagoda and the Shanxxi Museum. Exploration by bike is especially easy due to the city bike scheme that is in place, providing an abundance of strategically sited access points.

This was in fact my first experience of a tandem. It was a revelation; the concept is great and allows all to participate, regardless of experience or ability. The only negative is that the rear rider can choose to pedal or not, dependent on their laziness level, take note Rosie who used this get-out-clause like an expert.

The 13.7 kilometres was achieved relatively easily and we all felt unusually refreshed from the experience, mainly because we didn't stretch ourselves and pedalled at a comfortably steady pace. This allowed us to immerse in the culture and history of the city, it's an unusual way to see the interaction between the modern and the traditional and I would recommend the ride to any visitors, whether cyclists or not.

Another woe on Chinese roads is the increasing problem of congestion with nearly a third of the world's fifty most congested cities being in China, according to a report released by TomTom, the global leader in navigational and mapping products, and based on GPS measurements from the company's traffic database. This is another example of the why the bicycle is a great, healthy and convenient alternative to the daily chaos on the urban roads.

Chengdu in Sichuan Province was the first mis-conception of the trip (no doubt it won't be the last) as I was expecting a small provincial city, although the population is 4.5million, that's four times the size of Birmingham. The first thing you notice as you approach the city is a collection of busy and noisy ring roads (there are three in total) but it's openly a bike friendly city. Even though, the weather is grey and slightly damp for the majority of the year, it's a city that most peoples travel through enroute to other destinations. Like with most Chinese cities it has a large amount of sectioned off 'bike only' lanes signed for use by bicycles but the local moped enthusiasts happily encroach.

The city is world famous for its connection to the Giant Panda and their sanctuary is only twenty to thirty minutes' drive from the centre of the city, so it's in easy reach by bike. Once you have negotiated the busy ring road, there is a conveniently located cycle lane which will take you directly to the entrance of the park. I immediately liked Chengdu, it possesses a bizarre European feel, wide open boulevards and chalet style buildings. The traffic didn't seem as overwhelming as Beijing or Xian and the bike was well represented.

Like in most places nobody wears a helmet and the attire is appropriate for the day ahead (no sign of any PPE), suits, overalls, shorts, traditional attire all appear popular. The pollution levels are significantly less, this was perfectly highlighted by the lack of face masks. The Sichuan region is renowned for its spicy cuisine, everything is cooked with chilli's, it's my kind of food, eye-wateringly hot, dry but always well presented and temptingly palatable. We departed Chendgu with a fondness and a small amount of trepidation, we were heading south towards the Yunnan and a more rural experience awaited. We were stepping into the unknown and we couldn't wait, our eyes wide open to a simpler and less complicated way of life.

We arrived in the Yunnan Province, the Han people are the main group but many counties have a big enough ethnic presence to give them autonomous status. The terrain varies from high, cold, steep mountains, down through rolling hills and broad plains and tall, steep limestone hills flanking magnificent riverbeds

Our first destination was Lijiang. Like Chengdu, it's famous for its close proximity to a world renowned tourist attraction, Tiger Leaping Gorge. We were staying in the Old Town, which is engrossed by tourists and bikes, it's a vivid web of intricate canals with the main focus and heartbeat being the old market square, once the haunt of the Naxi traders. Unfortunately it is now obsessed by modernity, in the guise of colourful souvenir shops, thankfully the impact on the overall experience is negligible and still offers emotional views of the formidable Yulong Xueshan (Jade Dragon Snow Mountain) The atmosphere of the narrow alleys, red lanterns and constant noise of commerce is consuming, this is the side of China I had been searching for since our arrival, it can become busy so an early start will reward with a less claustrophobic exploration. Unfortunately my cynical (British) nature had kicked in and I began to question the realism, Were these quite rickety looking buildings just created for the holiday industry? I sincerely hope this is not the case, as the relaxed, pleasant and traditional surroundings was a major highlight and rightly it was given UN World Heritage status in 1999. Tiger Leaping Gorge is around an hour to an hour and a half drive from Lijiang so it is possible to ride but I would suggest you get a bus or a taxi because on arrival you will have to walk some distance to see the gorge at its best. The gorge is an impelling experience, the constant rumble from the angry water as it negotiates its way through the vertiginous surroundings. A mystical feeling takes over as you approach the viewing platforms, the Shangri-la side in tantalising, touching distance. The gorge is recognised as one the world's deepest, it measures 16km long and 3900m from the waters of the Jinsa River to the mountains of Haba Shan. The gorge can be accessed from two distinct locations, Shangri-la and Lijiang sides. The latter is a much flatter gentler trek (especially for the elderly in our party) but longer. In comparison, the opposite (Shangri-la) side is shorter but steeper with a technical descent.

The Old Town in Lijiang is a great place to explore at night, the darkness creates a completely different atmosphere as low lights and excited red lanterns come alive with a crescendo of animated chatter and enthusiastic bartering, and the bike is the ideal form of transportation. In spite of that, caution should be a priority unless you want to find yourself falling foul to one of the many drainage channels. Extra care should be taken at night as the street lighting is limited.

Dali is a mere two hours away by train and was a surprise, it's seemingly bike savvy, around every corner is a bike hire outlet. Once the original backpack hangout, the Bei town is the essence of the Yunnan. In the past the tourists have flocked to the area in the hope of finding themselves; nowadays, there are significantly less westerners heading here, so you are likely to experience a taste of the real China. The city and old town are absorbed by Erhai Lake and sit in the shadows of some riveting mountain ranges. The lake is a great place to pedal especially with the cool breeze which blows through the plateau. You can pedal around the whole lake which is called the 'Erhai Ring Road' encountering a selection of lovely villages. There are plenty of bike hire outlets dotted around the water. Enjoy watching the cormorant fisherman plying the trade on the water, the understanding between bird and man is so compelling, and is a dramatic symbol of the real China. The east side of the lake is classed as very much rugged and the west side is compelled by some mesmeric traditional villages. Dali is located west of Cangshan Mountain and east of Erhai Lake and was originally built during the Hongwu period of the Ming Dynasty with a rich history of over 600 years. Our hotel was located just off the famous Foreigner Street with its mystical eastern charms blended seamlessly with a chic western style, an evocative concoction of slate roads, numerous street vendors overwhelming the senses and the flow of water, it's easy to get lost in an ancient world. The main staple is bean and mushroom and I was exposed to my first taste of Taro which considering its bland appearance was incredibly delicious.

Close to the old town and just a short bike ride is the magical 'Three Pagodas' which is a masterpiece of ancient Chinese architecture and has stood for over a millennia. The experience is hypnotic, the Pagodas are so dramatic especially with the green mountains as a mesmerising backdrop. From the Bell Tower you can see an intoxicating panoramic vista of the Lake with again some rugged mountains enveloping the water, adding to overall effect. The Lake is only a short distance from the pagodas, locally the mountain is called the Black Dragon with green and the lake is the Half Moon with blue. According to legend, the lake has a gigantic jade cabbage on the bottom and this ensures the lake becomes white as jade. The lake is a substantial tourist attraction and consists of three islands, four continents, five lakes, nine bays and the Erhai Park. A boat trip is a must do, the surroundings so peaceful, promoting a mesmeric calm. Uniquely the boat's are guided gracefully through the fresh waters by women who are adorned in vibrantly decorated traditional attire, their age is inspiring, all appeared post retirement age but possessing an increased vigour and physical prowess which would embarrass many UK pensioners.

The lake is best accessed through the ancient village of Xizhou, which is one of China's most famous historical and cultural sites. The village is home to the Bei people and it retains many traditional Bei folk houses built in the Ming and Qing dynasty, the narrow evocative streets are the domain of the bicycle or moped, the car an occasional interloper. You can wander freely in and out of the old mansions and the Yan, Yang, Yin and Dong courtyards. Dali's relaxed, pragmatic atmosphere was a pleasant discovery and we will undoubtedly be returning, that I can assure you. Next stop Kunming, the capital of the Yunnan and a seven hour train journey from Dali.

Our arrival by train in Kunming was met with a chaos which we had previously not experienced on our journey. The hectic commerce from the colourful line of street vendors purveying all manner of local produce and the mass of vehicles creating a crescendo of noise. The humidity only accentuated a feeling of claustrophobia, well it is known as the 'Spring City' for its unchangeable climate. There is still a heavy military presence in and around the station following a high profile shooting near the transport hub in 2014. Once again, the bike and moped appeared a popular mode of transport with a constant procession of bikes weaving fastidiously through endless traffic servicing the train station. Once away from the mêlée, the traffic relented and the cycle lanes became king, their convenience and relative safety an overwhelming draw. The city and its suburbs is home to 7.2 million people, unfortunately it no longer has an old town, it's completely browbeaten by the metallic clean lines of skyscrapers and shopping malls.

Our stay in the city was brief, the next morning our Yunnan road trip began. We were heading for the Nine Dragons waterfall with a stopover in the nearby town of Luoping. The four hour drive was lengthy and bumpy so it's unrealistic to attempt by bike. In and around the waterfall is a great place to pedal a bike, the scenery is magical, the surroundings dominated by a collection of grass laden mountains ranging through several shades of lush green and quiet bucolic roads. The local farmers cultivate small plots of land, laid out in a patchwork of colours, squashed tightly into the hillsides, it must present a daily headache but they cope admirably. Despite the rapid growth and progress in China, life here is pastoral. A few visitors contribute to the tranquility, mist envelopes the mountains. It's a different matter in the summer, as the surroundings are mobbed by tourists.

The area has plenty of scenic locations on offer, one of my favourites is the Duoyi River and its water wheels. The Duoyi is a lovely tributary of the Nanpang River and turns up onto the hills to the tantilising reservoir at Lubuge. This area is home to the Buyi people and their prowess at farming both flat lands and hill slopes is evident all around. The fervently dressed women assume most of the agricultural duties and the men put their hands to construction work, ploughing and fishing. The river is easily accessible by bike, the route has many undulating sections, but the climbs won't cause much problem to a frequent cyclist, and the dramatic views of the lush landscape is a worthy recompense, notably the intricately manicured rice terraces.

Rennes, the city and the Tour (July 2015)

Out of the blue, one of my writers had asked if I would like to join a group of journalists on a trip to Rennes, the reason was two-fold: to discover the city and then watch Stage eight of the Tour depart the city. The itinerary as always appeared chaotic, depart Southend-on-Sea airport for a short flight to Rennes on the Friday, explore, relax and then on the Saturday immerse in the pandemonium of the TDF before returning that evening. It would be a novelty for me, my travels (of which there are many) invariably last much longer and keep me from my family, who I adore and miss immensely. It's a concept that you only recognise when you travel a lot.

The lure of the tour is global, I was asked last year (even though I was on my honeymoon, tut-tut) to do a radio interview for BBC World Service about the attraction and ultimate effect the race has on the people who are exposed to its phenomenon. At this stage the race was heading for Pall Mall and the capital, already leaving an infectious memory and legacy in the Yorkshire countryside.

Everybody is aware of the race, it's brand is known worldwide and generally the majority acknowledge the pain and dedication these amazing athletes have to endure to be a success, or just simply complete the event.

It would be my first visit to Rennes, the city is located in the north west portion of France and the capital and power house of Brittany region and at the heart of the Ille-et-Vilaine department. It has been a strategic point since the first century B.C as it lies on a promontory at the confluence of the Ille and Vilaine rivers. As always I tried to banish any pre-conceptions but is was difficult because I had only recently returned from a trip to Laval in the neighbouring Mayenne department, so the obvious comparisons would be made, how ever hard I tried.

Due to my wedding last year and subsequent honeymoon I had missed the Yorkshire Grand Départ and the UK's interaction with the race, obviously, being the good husband that I am. So the chance to catch the race on French soil was a wonderful opportunity, to simply smell the tension, the expectation and excitement was a chance I couldn't or wouldn't miss. It would also be my first (virgin-like) experience of the event in person, my previous interactions were through the brilliant coverage afforded by ITV4 or Eurosport.

Southend-on-Sea airport, as you can imagine, is small in stature but provides an essential transport alternative for the people of Essex and the East Coast. The main carrier is Stobart Air in conjunction with FlyBe, with regular routes to Rennes and a selection of other European destinations. The airport was quiet, the queues for check-in non-existent, it was a great relaxing alternative to any others means of transportation I have experienced for some time. Usually I find the whole airport experience evokes apprehension and a rather rushed frustration.

The flight always gives me the opportunity to apply my nerdy disposition and read up on the area, so, as I pawed over the contents of my Rough Guide to Brittany and Normandy (which I discovered the dog had ripped to shreds, a totally whole new meaning to the dog ate my homework), I was astonished to find that the majority of its fine medieval buildings were destroyed in 1720 when a drunken carpenter managed to decimate a large section of the city. The fire lasted a week and unfortunately only a small part of the city was left untouched. In 1724, Jaques Gabriel, architect to the king was given the responsibility of rebuilding and restoring the city to its past glories. Brittany and its close neighbour Normandy possess a strong individuality, similar to that of the Cornish, with the local dialect – Breton – spoken by the locals. However, the main language is French and a visitor is unlikely to encounter the local lingo. Barcelona is touched by Gaudi, Rennes is touched by Odorico, who has left his mark and legacy on the city, dominated by his unique façades, floors and World renowned mosaics.

After a smooth transition through baggage claim and customs (to be honest it was deserted), our hectic itinerary began almost immediately. After a short taxi ride we arrived in the old part of the city, the sun was buoyant, the sky neglected of any cloud cover. The hotel's central location was ideal, conveniently sat in the mix of everything. After some time to freshen up, we met with Andrey from Rennes Tourisme. She had arranged for us to hire bikes from 'Le Vélo Star', the city's popular bike scheme. The service is easy to use, the concept similar to the one adopted in London. The initiative has eighty-three stations dotted at strategic spots across the city, with over nine hundred bikes available, twenty-four seven.

Our guide was Dominque; her English as expected was exemplary. The riding was secondary to the acquisition of history; we were immersed in the heritage of the city as she delivered an eclectic mix of history and humour. Around every corner was an aspect of a building or legacy of past exploits that she detailed so vividly, it transformed you to that time. Considering its small size (compared to other French historic domains), there is plenty to see: the Cathedral, the old city walls, the market halls (based on Les Halles in Paris), and a collection of absolutely sublime half-timbered houses. Everywhere there was a constant reference to the deep affiliation with the Breton lifestyle, be it a small flag fluttering from a small window to an ostentatious carved emblem of loyalty, they were obviously proud of their Celtic heritage, and rightly so. Young and old were also very vocal of their hatred of King Louis XIV.

After our exertions, we retired to a traditional Breton hostelry to partake in the local produce. A mix of alcohol and hot beverages were consumed, some unfortunately spilt. The chat was inspiring; an underlying childish humour was rampant. Great people, great atmosphere, great coffee and a great setting.

That evening we feasted in the stunning Crêperie St George, the traditional façade hid a surprising modern décor, splashes of purple, inspired placement of chandeliers and a host of kooky accessories uplifted the space. The menu's theme was a play on the name 'George' with examples like a 'George Patten' and 'George Pompidou'', the fillings were a diverse mix of the expected, like ham and cheese and the obscure, black pudding and apple puree. I was assured that the 'Pompidou' was a great choice.

The night was still young, so we went off to explore the city by night. Between 1 July and 23 August, it hosts the 'Les Tombées de la Nuit', an illuminating light show which is not uncommon across France. Several of the city's most prominent and attractive buildings are visually transformed by a simple hypnotic kaleidoscope of colours; accompanied by music, it is a delight. The masses appeared dumbstruck by the show, or was it the free flowing alcohol on offer, al fresco style, from the multitude of bars and restaurants?

The sedate blasé approach to the itinerary was an inspired decision, it allowed for complete immersion in the culture, the people and the beautiful setting. The slightly rebellious dereliction of urgency was profound; we meandered, sauntered, plodded and crawled through the cobbled streets. The city's layout and small epicentre was easily orientated on foot, even easier on the bike, although the mass of cobbles may present a bone-shaking problem for the infrequent cyclist. Motor vehicles and public transport were practically unseen; the pedestrian was certainly king, especially in the Place de Lices and around the more popular historic sights.

Next morning, we met Lionel, another amiable guide; his task was to introduce us to the local markets. As well as the stone built Les Halles bustling with commerce, the streets in and around our hotel were over-run with stalls, fruit and veg crates discarded in a rather artistic fashion. The aromas attacked my senses, a cocktail of fresh fish, local ciders, cheese and a wonderful explosion of vibrant vegetables. It created a vibrant canvas to display the delicious local produce. The theme continued seamlessly as we explored the mass of flowers, it was definitely miles away from the good natured socialising only several hours earlier.

Lionel left us on Rue de Charles de Gaulle, at the starting point of Stage Eight of the Tour de France. The place was a throng of bodies all attired in their favourites riders colours, the noise was deafening, a constant melody dominated by the rather in tune Eritreans. As the entourage of teams buses and cars descended on the city, a controlled chaos took over. These athletes are looked upon as gods by many; there is mass hysteria as they teasingly emerge from the bus to speak to a TV crew and sign autographs before a hasty retreat back into the safety of the team bus. It was a wonderful experience, allowing me an insight into the amount of support the riders have to make the race a reality and a success, without their endeavours there would be no race.

The race departed with the usual crescendo and exuberant razzmatazz, the masses dispersed quickly, the souvenir outlets brimming with happy, Euro waving customers. Within minutes, the roads were deserted once more, the streets clear of rubbish or any sign of TDF paraphernalia.

Lunch was provided at the exquisite l'Amiral restaurant, recommended for its fish dishes, so I obviously opted for the steak. The sun was present but not as intrusive, we sat outside, as did all the diners. Suddenly, I was presented with the largest single piece of meat I have encountered (on a plate). It was cooked to perfection, this tender slab was succulently palatable, the flavour enhanced with the accompanying kick of creamy pepper sauce. Dessert was inconceivable and after a caffeine pick me up, we departed sluggishly. The itinerary had several suggestions to occupy the hours, such as the Thabor gardens or the Musée des Beaux-Arts, but, following our sizeable lunch, we were all overwhelmed by a lethargic general malaise. The only logically and preferred option was to recline in the deckchairs on Place de la Mairie. It was a great idea and a great location, sandwiched between the ostentatious Hôtel de Ville and the opera building, ideal for watching the world and people go past. There was no looking back, as soon as my bum touched the green fabric, I was semi-conscious and no doubt snoring followed.

The city's medieval quarter is referred to as 'La Ville Rouge', the highlight and epicentre is the evocative 'Place de Lices'. It happily accommodates a beautiful collection of (not as old as they appear) medieval façades, but who cares? These seventeenth century buildings provide Rennes with a glimpse into its past and allows both visitors and locals to connect with the great history, experiences and diverse cultures the city has been exposed to over its complicated existence. It was great to discover, a not so publicised part of the city's past, courtesy of Lionel on a walk Sunday morning. He explained our accommodation (Hôtel des Lices) is sat on the old site of the public executions, extremely popular in their day, morbid lot. Directly opposite is once the home of a lady serial killer, who, it's believed, poisoned sixty people, and, a short walk away, is the old prison, which hasn't changed visually since its incarceration days, apart from the surprising fact that nowadays it's home to a disco and a selection of bars. How convenient. Thankfully the legacy of misery and pain has now been replaced by a vibrant cosmopolitan air. Old town and new town, there was an obvious visual distinction, the simple difference in the construction of the façades, the medieval timber framed buildings and the pale stone built newer re-developments. Thankfully neither seemed out of place, they married together. As we searched for local produce in the guise of all butter biscuits and alcohol, I stumbled on a common sight nowadays throughout Europe, a shop dedicated to Ireland, a retail temple to all things Celtic. The owner was an affable guy, with a strange accent, a melodic mix of strong French with the occasional slip into a softer Dublin tone. This was understandable as he explained he had spent many years in Dublin. The undertones of a Celtic heritage dominated, the shop window proudly displayed a flag adorning all the Celtic nations, Scotland, Wales, Ireland, Isle of Man, Breton and Cornwall. The stock was a mixture of Irish and UK food items as well as a substantial clothing range. It had only been thirty-six hours since I left the UK but the sight of a Curly Wurly was too much to take, I was salivating uncontrollably.

The only disappointment was that I didn't get to try la galette-saucisse, a local delicacy consisting of a sausage in a buck wheat pancake, best accompanied with a dollop of mustard, the Breton version of a hot dog with a touch of 'Je ne sais quoi'. Maybe next time!